Chicken
ON THE MENU

Luc Hoornaert and Kris Vlegels

LANNOO

Mechelse Wyandotte – 20th Generation Cosmopolitan Chicken Project © Koen Vanmechelen

Chicken on the menu

Without chicken, humankind would never have become the species it now is: the top of the food chain. And vice versa. Alongside humankind, chicken has spread all over the world and its diversity has increased enormously. For thousands of years, the range of human cultures has not only found its counterpart in the biology of the chicken, but certainly also in the nutritional importance of our most important 'companion animal'.

This book is a magnificent illustration of this interdependence. It reflects our various cultural individualities as well as the beauty created when local characteristics merge in a broad world view. It links tradition to the present day and to a clear vision of the future which, I am convinced, will be based on sustainable food and the right outcome of global versus local.

Koen Vanmechelen,
artist and former chef

TABLE OF CONTENTS

    5 Foreword by Koen Vanmechelen

9. THE NETHERLANDS
- 9 **Boys are lucky**
- 9 **Nel Schellekens**
- 13 Haycock... a country cockerel
- 14 Elderberry cockerel (floral cockerel)... with 'hidden' floral apple sauce
- 16 Gizzards on potato scones with quick pickle
- 18 Chicken, cockscomb and testicle salad
- 20 Bouchée au roi
- 22 Pategg' – or pâté in egg

24. ITALY
- 25 **Chicken, chicken, chicken, where are you?**
- 27 **Felice Miluzzi**
- 28 Biancomangiare alla veneziana
- 31 Pollo alla diavola
- 33 Pollo alla romana
- 34 Pollo in pancetta
- 36 Pollo alla cacciatora

38. JAPAN
- 39 **Meanwhile in Japan ...**
- 45 **Dimitri Proost**
- 46 Yakitori
- 49 Toriwasa
- 50 Tsukune
- 53 Tori no karaage
- 55 Mizutaki
- 57 Tsubu-miso gako hinadori no oven yaki
- 59 Soboro don

60. CHINA
- 61 **Wang Rong Chick Chick...**
- 63 **Leung Kwai Lam**
- 65 Bo bo Chicken
- 66 Stuffed chicken
- 69 Thai-style chicken legs
- 71 Xiao Lung Pao
- 73 Little chicken curry dumplings
- 75 Stuffed steamed bamboo fungi

76. KOREA
- 77 **Jinjuu before swine**
- 81 Korean double fried chicken

82. INDIA
- 83 **Mandelbrot**
- 87 **Hariprasad Shetty**
- 88 Tandoori Chicken
- 90 Kip saag
- 92 Chana aur khatte pyaaz ka murgh
- 94 Garlic Naan
- 95 Chicken Tikka and Naan Wrap with Mint Chutney
- 97 Murg do pyaaza

98. UK
99 **And now for something completely different**
101 **Heston Blumenthal**
104 Chicken liver parfait
107 Chicken Caesar Salad
109 Roast chicken and sage stuffing
110 Chicken and grape stove pot
113 **Michael Yates**
114 Tandoori poussin

116. BBQ
117 **The first pitmasters were woman**
118 The flying chicken
121 **Matthias Jacobs & Vadim Vesters**
122 Southern pride smoked wings
124 Pulled chicken sandwich
126 Beercan chicken
129 Chicken on asado cross

130. LATIN AMERICA
131 **Barbecue vs Barbacoa**
135 **Bart Huybrechts**
136 Mole poblano basis
136 Pollo con mole
138 Sticky chili chicken wings
140 Empanadas with chicken liver and mole poblano
143 Chicharron de pollo
144 Sopa de patas

146. CLASSIC DISHES
149 **Patrick Verheire**
150 Casserole of sautéed chicken with artichoke, sage and preserved lemon
152 Fillet of poulet de Bresse, asparagus, peas and chanterelle mushrooms
154 Creamy chicken soup and lobster bisque
156 Pozharsky made with Poulet de Bresse, braised chicory and Pommes Anna
158 Salad with blond chicken livers, coated with sirop de Liège and green beans
160 **Henk Van Oudenhove**
162 Poulet de Bresse 'en galantine'
167 **Steven Naessens**
168 Poulet de Bresse with Vin Jaune and morels
171 **Johan Segers**
172 Chicken in pig's bladder
174 Fresh pasta with cockscombs, chicken liver, stomach, heart and fresh morels
177 Financière en feuilleté au brun
179 Chicken liver and crayfish flan
180 Chicken salad with cepsμ
183 **Filip Slangen**
184 Coq au vin
186 Roast chicken with lemon and rosemary
189 Poussin en sarcophage
191 **David Martin**
193 Fuck you chicken
195 Sot-l'y-laisse (chicken oysters) with preserved garlic
197 Chicken marinated in shio koji and grilled over charcoal
198 Chicken in a cocoa and coffee crust
201 Whole chicken poached in artisan butter
203 Chicken on a spit

206. ADDRESSES

BOYS ARE LUCKY

If you are born as a male animal in our part of the world you are lucky because, as a rule, people mostly eat female animals. Females are just more cost-effective (female calves will produce milk later on and give birth to more calves – hens lay eggs, and so on...). We apparently think it costs too much to rear a profitable male and release it into the food chain.

Nel Schellekens thinks differently. She thinks that people ought to eat everything and not cherry-pick so fussily. Why should a bent asparagus stem be worth less than a straight one? Why don't we eat meat from male animals as we used to? The arrogance of the contemporary consumer apparently has no limits. An awareness campaign by the government is urgently needed to give people a wake-up call. Or is it normal that almost all young cockerels disappear into the gas chamber immediately after being born, going from there via the shredder to become a source of protein for farmed salmon? Complete madness.

Chicken with balls

Meat from cockerels is tasty and nutritious, but it tastes and feels totally different to meat from hens. The chef must use his experience and adjust the method of preparation to ensure that the meat is good to eat.

A chef with balls

Nel Schellekens is a truly phenomenal person with drive to match a Duracell Bunny. She is a veritable missionary for nose-to-tail eating. Fergus Henderson from London, the other star of this movement, might be the uncrowned king, but Nel is the queen. She is genuinely a woman on a mission: a mission to disseminate delicious food. She lives for delicious food herself and it makes her profoundly happy. Nel is Slow Food, but at a gallop. I sometimes wonder where she gets all her energy to keep fighting such a losing battle against mass consumption.

She is a whirlwind that never seems to abate, but in the midst of this apparent chaos and commotion, she still manages to find the peace and focus to cook an essential dish. She was of course almost literally brought up cooking. Her Aunt Anneke got her to chop off young cockerels' heads and clean them out completely when she was a

Nel Schellekens had to chop off cockerels' heads and clean them out completely when she was a child. Her principle of never throwing anything away dates back to those days.

child. Her principle of never throwing anything away dates back to those days.

She is keen to share her passion for delicious food with everyone. She reigns over her underrated restaurant, De Gulle Waard in Winterswijk. It is a real pleasure to see a chef at work who knows where she has come from, where she is now and where she wants to go. She has her very own style in the kitchen and that creates a measure of calm. The creative process takes place deep in her heart and soul and is not dependent on any high tech demo by a conceited tattooed chef at a hot-shot culinary fair. Preparing a meal is a natural process of evolution and the sharing of skills.

Nel is undoubtedly one of the most underrated chefs I know but she is gathering a following and touching a chord with her purity.

Michelin man

The laying hen's little brother. No, it's not fat, but it does taste very good. This gentleman cockerel has the unique characteristic of blowing itself up like a Michelin man when cooking. Its thin skin bulges alarmingly, but it won't burst. And it stays that way until you open the oven...

Gizzards

Gésiers – as they call preserved gizzards in France – are a delicacy. Birds have a muscular stomach called a gizzard. Their food enters through the crop. From there it goes through to the gizzard where it is kneaded and ground before entering the digestive system. That is why a chicken's stomach is a muscle, just like the heart. It also has the structure of a muscle.

Cleaning gizzards

A muscular stomach has two compartments held together by a thick yellow skin. If you need to clean them yourself, first cut the stomach in two. Remove the food that is usually still in there. Rinse well. Now cut off the two bundles of muscles to the left and right behind a membrane. You can't miss them; they are like red diamonds. Now remove all the membrane.

'Salad of chicken, cockscombs and cockerels' testicles'. Hmm. This certainly isn't your everyday dish. A long time ago it would have been though.

Cookery books of yesteryear contained many recipes for cockscombs. A famous one is what was known as the queen's titbit adorned by the comb as a crown. (See recipe *bouchée au roi* on page 20)

Another interesting cockscomb fact: a comb is rich in hyaluronic acid. This endogenous substance increases the elasticity of the skin and the mobility of joints. Hyaluronic acid is frequently used to combat the aging process. It can be swallowed and injected: it is used in fillers for lip augmentation, for instance. So, perhaps eating a cockscomb might help too?

HAYCOCK... A COUNTRY COCKEREL

INGREDIENTS

- handful of unsprayed hay for stuffing and optionally putting in the pan
- 1 cockerel
- casserole or a cedar wood box
- 1/2 a bottle of beer
- salt and pepper
- 1 sour apple and/or lemon, in pieces
- oil infused with chopped fresh thyme and, for garlic-lovers, some crushed garlic

METHOD

Method

Soak some hay (as much as will fit inside the cockerel) in beer. Do that a day in advance if possible, because it will make the hay softer and easier to stuff inside the cockerel. Season the cockerel inside and out to taste.

Once the hay is soft, squeeze it out a bit and mix some pieces of sour apple and/or lemon through it. Stuff the seasoned cockerel with as much as will fit.

1. **Two methods**
   Big Green Egg or other barbecue with a lid:

   Place the cockerel on a tray/dish/pan filled with some hay that has been soaked in beer. Sprinkle the cockerel with the flavoured oil.

2. **Oven:**

   Place the cockerel on some hay in a casserole and place some beer in an oven-proof bowl next to it to keep it moist. Cover the casserole. After 25 minutes, remove the lid from the casserole and baste the cockerel with some oil.

   Let it brown without the lid.

   The cockerel will take 30-40 minutes to cook at 180 °C using either method.

ELDERBERRY COCKEREL (FLORAL COCKEREL)... WITH 'HIDDEN' FLORAL APPLE SAUCE

Cockerel is delicious with flowers such as elderberry, but other flowers, (such as roses) are equally good.

INGREDIENTS

- 1 cockerel
- salt and pepper
- sour apples, as many as are need to stuff the cockerel
- sprigs of elderberry, including for a garnish
- elderberry syrup

METHOD

Season the cockerel inside and out with salt and pepper.

Cut the apples into pieces and remove the cores. Destem the elderberry flowers and mix them with some elderberry syrup and the apples. This will be the hidden apple sauce. Use enough syrup to dampen the pieces of apple. Too much syrup will make the stuffing soggy. Stuff the cockerel with the mixture. Roast in the oven at 180 °C for 30-40 minutes.

Replace the burnt sprigs of elderberry with fresh elderberry flowers to serve.

Treat!

Chicken with chips and apple sauce isn't only a treat for children.

Note:
Chicken always needs something acidic to keep it as tender as possible.
Citrus fruit can be used, of course, but sour apples are an excellent alternative. Chicken and other poultry is cooked when its core temperature reaches 75 °C measured at the thickest part of the inner thigh.

NETHERLANDS

GIZZARDS ON POTATO SCONES WITH QUICK PICKLE

INGREDIENTS

Gizzard
- 25 g sea salt
- 3 g cane sugar
- 2 g coriander seeds
- small piece of star anise
- 3 cracked black peppercorns
- goose fat *(for preserving)*

Potato scones
- 3 eggs *(approx. 60 g yolk and approx. 100 g white)*
- 250 g boiled and mashed floury potatoes
- 80 g plain flour
- 150 ml milk
- pinch of pepper
- salt and nutmeg to taste
- oil

Quick pickle
- 100 ml water
- 100 ml vinegar
- 100g sugar
- seasoning such as mustard seed, peppercorns, fennel seed, thyme, etc.
- 1 shallot, in rings
- 1 spring onion, in rings
- 1 small carrot, sliced
- 1 fresh gherkin or piece of cucumber, cubed *(or other vegetables such as cauliflower florets, beans, etc.)*

METHOD

Dry gizzard pickle

Make a dry pickle by mixing all the ingredients (except the fat) together. Rub the dry pickle into the gizzards.
Roll them up tightly in cling film or create a vacuum and leave them to soak up the pickle overnight.
Rinse them in cold water the following day until they are completely pliable again (the pickle will make them hard). Refresh the water a few times.

Preserving

Place the gizzards in a small pan or an oven dish. Pour over enough goose fat to cover them completely. Place them in the oven heated to just under 100 °C for about four hours.

Potato scones

Separate the eggs. Beat the egg whites until stiff.
Make a batter with the egg yolks, potato, milk and spices; fold it into the beaten egg whites.
Heat the oil in a non-stick pan. Fry spoonfuls of the batter to make mini scones.

Quick pickle

Mix the water, vinegar and sugar together and bring to the boil. Add as much seasoning as you wish. Leave to infuse for 10 minutes.
Now add the chopped vegetables. Bring back to the boil. Remove the pan from the heat and leave the vegetables to cool in the liquid.

Plating up

Lay a few pieces of gizzard (hot or cold) on each scone; pour a spoonful of vinaigrette on top.

Note:
Re-use the liquid from the pickle (gherkin, onions) from your fridge.
Bring the liquid to the boil and pickle the vegetables in it.

SALAD OF CHICKEN, COCKSCOMBS AND COCKERELS' TESTICLES

INGREDIENTS

Cockscombs
12 cockscombs ·
chicken stock, enough to cover the cockscombs ·
(highly seasoned court bouillon can also be used)

Marinade
1 small onion, shredded ·
300 ml redcurrant juice ·
(cherry juice is also delicious and a good red colour too)
3 cloves ·
1 bay leaf ·
50 ml vinegar ·
1 Tbsp. honey ·
50 ml water ·
freshly ground black pepper ·
a little oil ·

Vinaigrette
2 Tbsp. mustard ·
200 ml syrup (see above) ·
0.5 litre oil *(a combination of two parts rapeseed oil, two parts sunflower oil and one part nut oil is delicious)*
5 shallots, chopped very finely ·
freshly ground salt and pepper ·

Salad
as many cockerels' testicles as you want ·
about 100 g cockscomb mushrooms ·
(or more if you like of course)
splash of oil for frying ·
mesclun *(e.g. mustard greens, beet greens, rocket, mizuna, spinach leaves, chives, chervil and dill)* ·
chopped, roasted hazelnuts ·
(roasted buckwheat is also delicious)
flowers such as those from chives or marigolds, etc. ·

METHOD

Preparation

Clean the combs by removing the gristle if necessary. That is what attaches it to the head.

Place the combs in salted water or salted milk for a few hours to rinse them clean. Squeeze them out to check that the water is clear; if so, they are clean.

Put the cockscombs on to boil in cold chicken stock. Bring to the boil and simmer for about one hour. Do not boil.

Sometimes the comb's epidermis will come loose; remove it if it does.

Retain the cooking liquid for the cock's testicles.

Marinade

Fry the onion in some of the oil. Add the juice as soon as it starts to change colour. Reduce the juice down to half its volume by boiling it with the other ingredients until it is syrupy. Place the combs in the syrup and cook for 10 minutes; leave them in the syrup to cool. The syrup is the basis for the vinaigrette.

Vinaigrette

Stir the mustard into the syrup until smooth. Add the oil, stirring continuously.

Add the shallots. Season to taste with salt and pepper.

Salad

Poach the cockerels' testicles in the same hot stock. They are ready when they feel firm.

Fry the cockscomb mushrooms in the hot oil until crispy. Add the cooked cockerel testicles too if you like.

Plating up

Make up the salad with the cockscomb mushrooms and cockerel testicles. Drizzle with the vinaigrette. Sprinkle a few hazelnut crumbs on top. Decorate with some flowers.

BOUCHÉE AU ROI

A male variation of the delicious *bouchée à la reine,* or vol-au-vent made from a cockerel with a cockscomb and other parts of the cockerel.

INGREDIENTS

- 50 g butter
- 50 g plain flour
- 0.5 litre cold sieved chicken stock, or better, cockerel stock
- cooked pieces of cockerel meat and optionally cockscomb
- mushrooms of similar sizes, finely chopped *(other mushrooms can be used)*
- cockscombs and cockerels' testicles *(see page 18)*
- 100 ml cream
- 1 egg yolk
- salt and pepper to taste
- puff pastry vol-au-vents

METHOD

Heat the butter in a pan. Do not allow to brown. Cook the mushrooms in the butter. Stir in the flour a little at a time and cook for a minute. Taste to check that the floury taste has gone. Gradually pour in the cold stock, stirring continuously until the sauce is smooth.

Add the cooked cockerel meat to the sauce. Beat the egg yolk and the cream together. Stir it into the sauce, but do not allow it to boil again.

Season to taste with salt and pepper.

Spoon into the gently warmed vol-au-vents. Place the cockscombs on top and a testicle here and there.

'PATEGG' – OR PÂTÉ IN EGG

It's possible to cut the top off a raw egg straight across with a very sharp knife. The eggshell needs to be completely clean and sterile. Do this by boiling the shells. The membrane can then be easily removed. Dry the eggshells and sterilise them in the oven at 100 °C for about 10 minutes. The eggshells will now keep well for a long time. Before filling them, however, heat them again to sterilise them. They look nice filled with egg salad or, as in this recipe, with pâté in egg. They make terrific containers for dips. No eggshells to hand? You can also use caul fat to make the pâté in.

INGREDIENTS

- for 500 g pâté, about 10 eggshells
- 2 eggs
- 200 g chicken livers, kidneys and heart, minced
- 200 g thigh meat, minced
- 2 shallots or onions, very finely shredded
- chives and little garlic, very finely shredded
- sour apple, chopped small
- 50 ml apple-flavoured gin or other Dutch gin or cognac
- a few drops of Worcester sauce
- dash of cream
- salt and pepper to taste

METHOD

Beat the eggs well in a bowl. Work quickly and keep them cold by placing the bowl over ice, for example.

Mix the minced meat with the onions, garlic, chives and apple. Knead lightly.

Mix in the alcohol and some Worcester sauce.

Add sufficient cream to make a creamy mixture.

Season to taste with salt and pepper.

Check for seasoning by frying a little bit of the mixture first. Only make sure it is cooked, don't really fry it. (Frying will give it quite a different flavour due to the Maillard reaction.)

Put the pâté mixture to one side and chill. Leaving it to rest will improve the flavour.

Pre-heat the oven to 170 °C.

Carefully grease the eggshells and fill them up to the brim with the pâté mixture. Place the filled eggshells in a cardboard egg box to hold them steady. Place the box on an oven-proof tray in a layer of water. The cardboard will soak up the water: a different but effective au-bain-marie method.

Put it straight into the oven. It will take about 25 minutes to cook. Very carefully, remove the soaking wet box out of the water and place it in ice-cold water. This will quickly cool the pateggs. They taste good hot too. Serve immediately in that case.

Presenting the pâté in the egg box looks great too. An attractive, tasty snack with crostini to serve with drinks.

NETHERLANDS

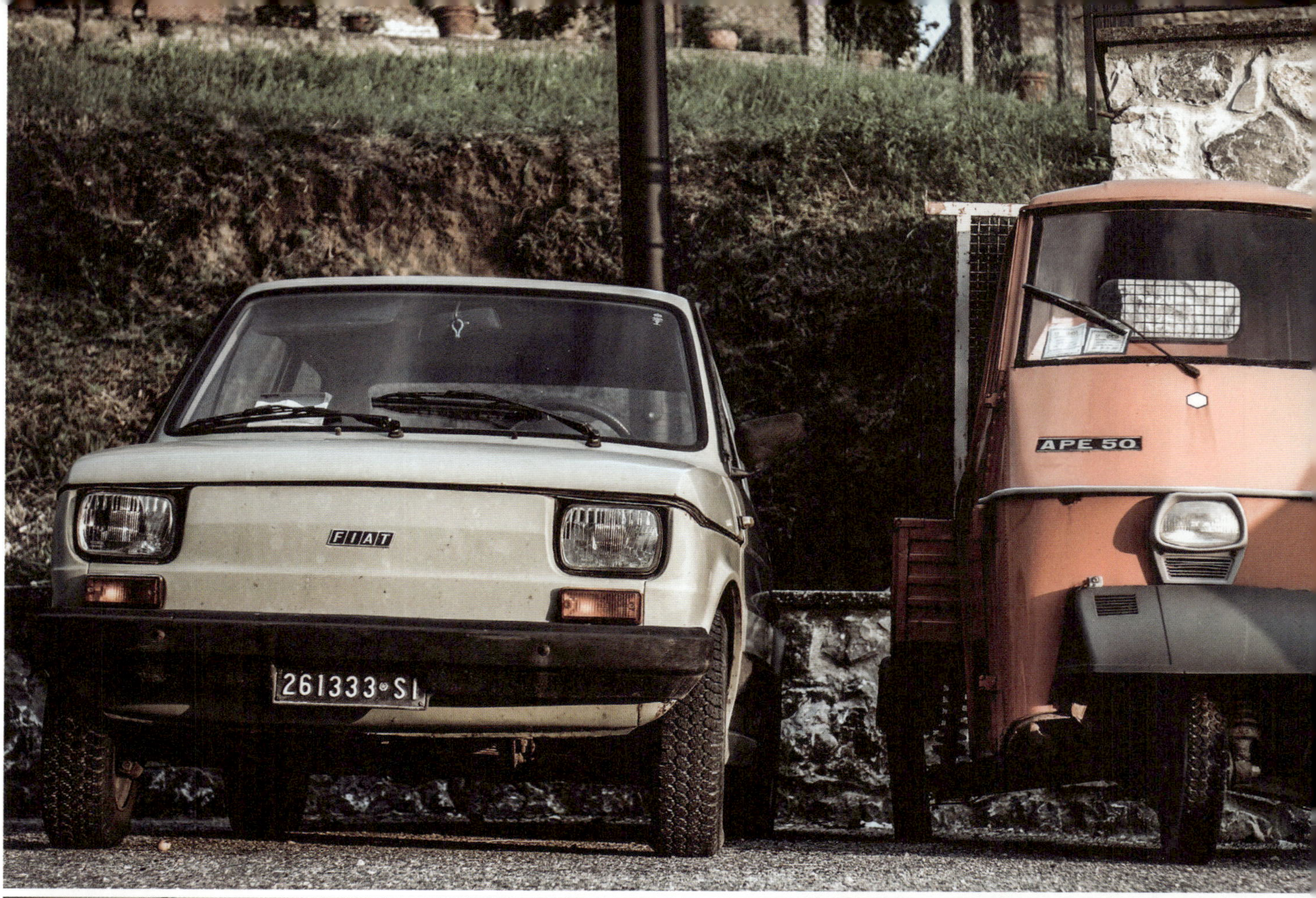
FIAT
261333 SI
APE 50

IOY DIVISION
RASTA!!
OMBOCLOT
FLIP

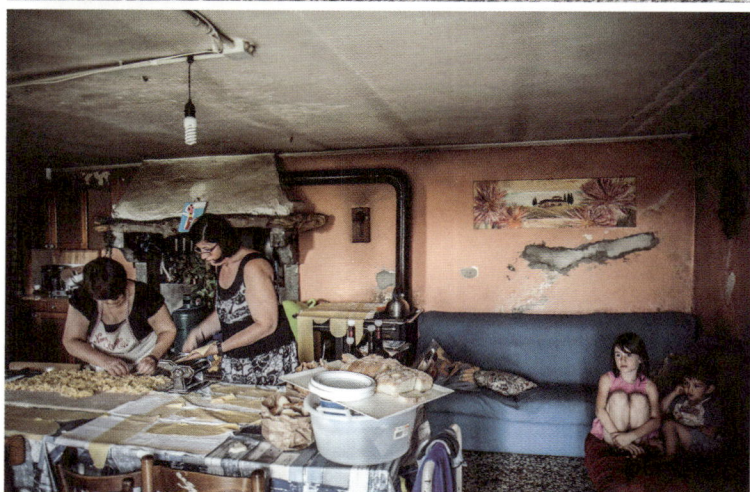

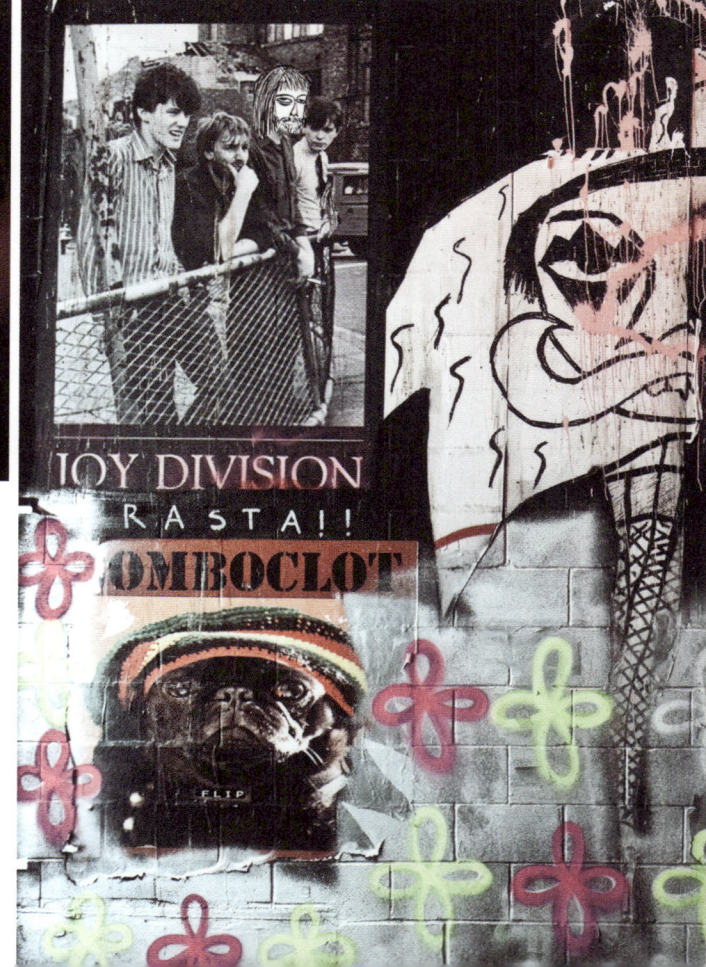

CHICKEN, CHICKEN, CHICKEN, WHERE ARE YOU?

The etched phrase in the runout groove on my original vinyl version of Joy Division's
Closer – one of my prized possessions – contains a few chicken tracks with the text
'Where has the chicken gone?'

I could swear that Massimo Bottura is a fan of Joy Division. This fantastic chef is among the world's great chefs and, as far as I am concerned, is in all senses the closest to being a contemporary artist. His dishes evolve and reveal a glimpse of the way he interprets feelings, memories and emotions. His daughter Alexa used to play with her toy kitchen for hours and when she served her father with a pile of plastic vegetables, he asked what this delicious meal was called. With a straight face, she replied: *'Chicken, chicken, chicken, where are you?'* They both dissolved in fits of laughter.

This popped back into his mind much later when he wanted to make a chicken salad with a very intense chicken flavour, but without a single trace of actual chicken. And so he made nine little piles of finely julienned vegetables in dense, intense chicken vinaigrette and when it was served he even sprayed it with roast chicken-flavoured 'eau de cologne'. And thus, chicken

ITALY

The tiny restaurant, Rossi, strongly reminiscent of Italy, sets the tone and is an oasis of Italian authenticity in Belgium.

Felice Miluzzi

can be everywhere and yet nowhere. This latest idea came from a bronze self-portrait of Alighiero Boetti. One of my great idols, Bruce Nauman, compares creating a work of art with a game, but a game in which – once you play it well – you can change the rules. And that is exactly Bottura's philosophy: you sometimes get astonishing results by changing conventions and rules, without deviating from your initial plan.

Felice Miluzzi

Italian cuisine is one of the few styles of cookery that can get right to the essence of the ingredients. It uses very few ingredients, but they are of a superior quality. That is the trademark of every self-respecting Italian chef. Italian cuisine seems to be easy to export: Italian restaurants can be found all over the world. Obviously an Italian chef is more than an Italian with an attitude in a chef's outfit. Besides having an irresistible flair, you certainly need a firm grounding and you need to have grown up in an environment in which the most important topic of conversation was the menu for the evening.

Felice Miluzzi was born in Grotti, a little farming village in Central Italy. He began his gastronomic voyage of discovery at a very young age on the family farm. His *nonna* Gina was intent on teaching little Felice everything about the distinction between good and bad products, and about the authenticity and wealth of Italy's edible flora and fauna. And that formed the basis for his current philosophy, which can best be described as luxury in simplicity, a mantra later confirmed and perfected by the experience he gained working for restaurateurs like Massimo Bottura. Let the main ingredient on the plate set the tone by emphasising its freshness and fundamental quality.

Miluzzi's tiny restaurant in Leuven, highly reminiscent of Italy, sets the scene and is an oasis of Italian authenticity in a country where more Pizza Hawaii is eaten than Pizza Margherita. Almost like a missionary, with Carlo Petrini's manifesto under his arm, Miluzzi preaches the cuisine of his Italy: no-fuss cookery but instead flavours, dedication and a lot of *amore*.

BIANCOMANGIARE ALLA VENEZIANA

BROMAGERE XIV-XV

INGREDIENTS

- 1 boiling hen weighing at least 1 kg
- 6 litres water
- 2 sticks of celery
- 2 cloves of garlic
- 6 cloves
- 1 onion
- 200 g peeled almonds
- 2 bay leaves
- 10 g white pepper
- 1 stick of cinnamon
- 100 g rice flour
- salt and pepper to taste

Garnish
- a few wild mint leaves
- a few toasted almond slivers
- croutons
- 1 tsp. olive oil

METHOD

Place all the ingredients apart from the rice flour in a pan and bring to the boil. Simmer very gently, boiling the liquid down to about two litres.

Turn off the heat and leave to rest for one hour. Sieve the mixture through a fine sieve and put it in the fridge for at least six hours.

Remove some chicken from the carcass and reserve for later, seasoned with some olive oil, salt and pepper.

Carefully remove the fat from the cooled mixture.

Bring to the boil and add the rice flour to thicken.

Add the reserved chicken and finish off with the almond slivers, the mint, the croutons and the olive oil.

POLLO ALLA DIAVOLA

INGREDIENTS

2 chickens ·
zest of one lemon ·
juice of one lemon ·
4 bay leaves ·
5 Tbsp. extra virgin olive oil ·
salt to taste ·
black pepper to taste ·

For the salad
an aromatic salad of rocket, watercress, ·
valerian, poached green beans,
poached cauliflower florets, al dente
olive oil ·
1 tsp. chili powder ·
1 tsp. sun-dried tomato puree ·
a few drops of balsamic vinegar ·

For the sweet and sour sauce
200 g *glace de volaille* ·
20 g tomato paste ·
1 tsp. chestnut honey ·
1 tsp. red wine vinegar ·
1 fresh chili pepper ·

METHOD

Debone the chicken, retaining the bones and try to keep the chicken intact. Marinate the meat in the lemon juice, the zest, the olive oil and the bay leaves (in a vacuum bag if possible) for at least 24 hours.

Pat the chicken dry.

Season the chicken with salt and pepper.

Fry the chicken, skin side down, cover with kitchen paper and place a weight on top for about five minutes until the skin is nice and crisp; turn the chicken over and fry without using the kitchen paper or weight.

Leave the chicken to rest for a few minutes.

Mix the ingredients for the sweet and sour sauce and bring to the boil.

Cut the chicken in half and serve with the aromatic salad which you have dressed with olive oil and balsamic vinegar and 1 tsp sun-dried tomato paste. Decorate the plate with some chili powder.

POLLO ALLA ROMANA

INGREDIENTS

2 chickens, cut into large portions ·
(thighs, wings, breast)
salt and pepper to taste ·
20 g garlic, finely chopped ·
100 g celery, finely chopped ·
olive oil ·
100 g onion, finely chopped ·
4 red peppers ·
4 sprigs of rosemary ·
1 glass of crisp dry white wine ·
200 ml San Marzano tomato pulp ·
100 g cherry tomatoes, halved ·

METHOD

Rub salt, pepper and half of the garlic into the chicken.

Fry the chicken portions on a high heat until they are crisp.

Gently fry the celery in a pan with olive oil; add the onion and then some garlic.

Add the fried chicken portions (but not the breast meat) to the pan with the chopped red pepper and continue to cook for 5 minutes; remove from the heat.

Add the rosemary and mix carefully.

Pour in the white wine and boil down gently. Add the San Marzano pulp and the cherry tomatoes with a glass of water; cover the pan with a lid and leave to cook for 25 minutes.

Now add the breast meat, cover again and leave to stand for five minutes. Remove the chicken and reduce the liquid until it resembles a sauce; replace the chicken before serving.

Almost like a missionary, with Carlo Petrini's manifesto under his arm, Miluzzi preaches the cuisine of his Italy: no-fuss cookery but instead flavours, dedication and a lot of *amore*.

POLLO IN PANCETTA

INGREDIENTS

- 4 boneless chicken legs
- 0.5 tsp. garlic, finely chopped
- 4 sprigs of rosemary, two of them chopped very finely
- salt and pepper to taste
- extra virgin olive oil
- 28 thin rashers of aged Tuscan pancetta
- 500 g new potatoes, sliced very thinly (0.5 cm)
- 2 cloves of garlic, crushed
- 100 g *glace de volaille*
- 20 mini carrots

METHOD

Lay seven rashers of pancetta on a chopping board and place a boneless chicken leg on top. Season with salt, pepper, garlic and the finely chopped rosemary and roll the chicken leg up in the pancetta. Do the same with the other chicken legs and put them all in the fridge for an hour.

Season the potatoes with salt, pepper, olive oil and the crushed garlic; place them in a casserole on top of the sprigs of rosemary.

Lay the chicken legs on top of the potatoes and cook in the oven at 180 °C for 30 minutes.

Fry the carrots in olive oil.

Place the potatoes on a plate and lay a chicken leg on top; pour a few spoonfuls of *glace de volaille,* brought up to boiling point, over the top. Decorate with the carrots.

POLLO ALLA CACCIATORA

INGREDIENTS

2 chickens, cut into large portions *(thighs, wings, breast)* ·
salt and pepper to taste ·
20 g garlic, finely chopped ·
100 g celery, finely chopped ·
1 carrot, finely chopped ·
extra virgin olive oil ·
50 g onion, finely chopped ·
1 sprig of rosemary, a few sage leaves, some thyme and 2 bay leaves ·
1 glass of dry red wine ·
100 ml San Marzano tomato pulp ·
100 cl cherry tomatoes, halved ·
100 g black olives ·
100 g dried funghi porcini, soaked overnight ·
100 g pancetta, sliced thinly ·
1 carrot ·

METHOD

Rub the salt, pepper and half of the garlic into the chicken.

Fry the chicken portions on a high heat until they are crisp.

Gently fry the celery in a pan with olive oil; add the onion and then the rest of the garlic.

Fry the chopped pancetta, add the celery and the carrot and continue to fry.

Add the chicken portions (apart from the breast meat) and cook for 5 minutes; remove from the heat. Add the rosemary, sage, thyme and bay leaves and mix thoroughly.

Add the red wine and boil the liquid down a little over a low heat.

Add the pulp and the fresh tomatoes, as well as the olives, the porcini and a glass of water (use the soaking liquid from the porcini).

Cover and cook for 25 minutes; add the breast meat and cook for another five minutes with the lid on.

Remove the chicken and reduce the liquid until it resembles a sauce; replace the chicken.

MEANWHILE IN JAPAN ...

As we walk through the maze of little streets in Tokyo it soon becomes clear that this city is a bit like a spider's web. Because only the main streets have real names, it's not very easy – especially for non-locals – to find your way around. After crossing a pedestrian bridge over a little stream, almost hidden behind a few buildings of course, we arrive at one of this fascinating city's chicken nirvanas, Akira in the Meguro-ku district.

Akira is a *yakitori,* a restaurant that specialises in chicken. The head chef learnt his craft in Japan's chicken capital, Yokohama, where he spent a long apprenticeship at the cult *yakitori,* Torigen. Being seemingly impossible to find is common to both restaurants and yet both are crammed every day. I am in search of *toriwasa,* a real speciality which is nowadays highly revered in Yokohama in particular, but actually also in any self-respecting *yakitori*. What I am specifically looking for is sashimi, or raw chicken in other words: breast, thighs, heart, liver and stomach. I would never take it into my head to order such a thing in the west, never mind eat it, but I feel safe in the hands of Japanese food experts.

Salmonella has of course been around for much longer than our discovery of it. But Japan is probably one of the last countries where raw food has been elevated to a true culinary art, and so it is safe. They have even recently switched to breeding Blue Foot chickens here, an extremely disease-resistant hybrid developed by a Canadian, Peter Thiessen. He bred this species as an alternative to the Bresse Gauloise, but when evidence emerged that the risk of infection was very low in this hybrid, it began to attract the attention of the Japanese market. When the entire Canadian Blue Foot chicken population was wiped out by bird flu in 2004, there were luckily still a few thousand left in California. Fans of Japanese *toriwasa* were able to breathe a sigh of relief.

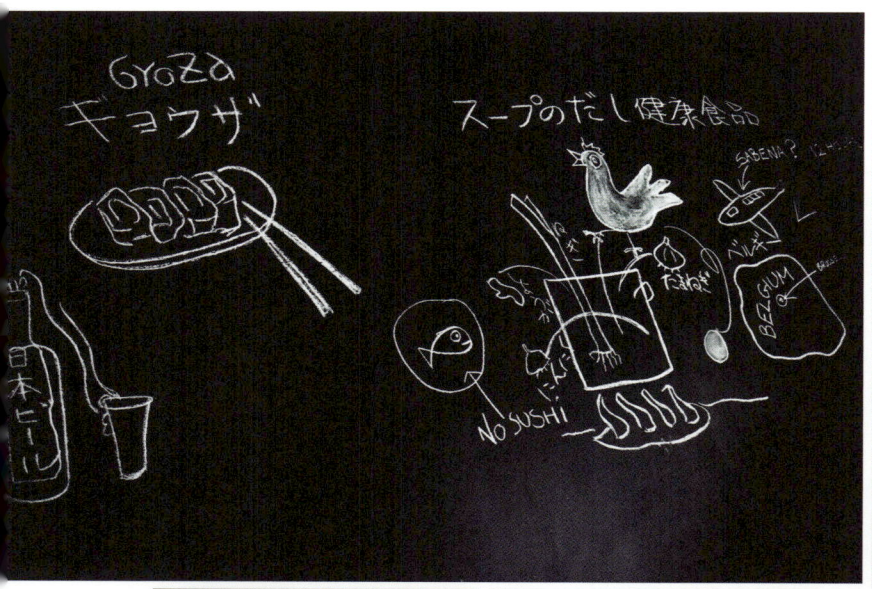

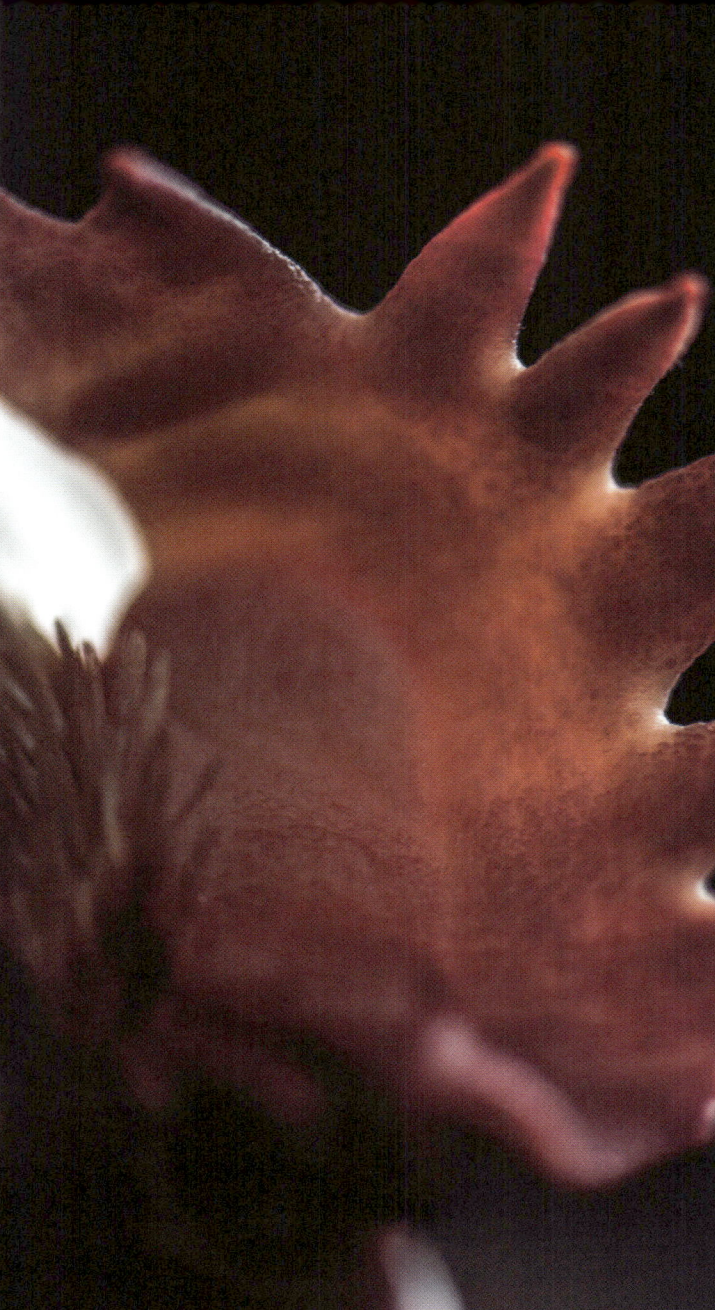

A chicken went to Japan...

The first mention of chickens in Japanese literature dates from the 8th century. There is no record of when the chicken appeared in Japan, but its introduction probably corresponded to the origins of and route taken by the Japanese people: from China via the Korean peninsula to Japan, and needless to say, all of that dates back much further. It can be assumed that chicken played a part in the Japanese diet right from the very start. Chicken hunting as a relic of old rituals does however appear in sources dating from around the year 300. Two ancient 8th-century stories, *Kojiki* and *Nihonshoki*, feature Tokoyonaga-nakidori. This sacred animal, actually a chicken, saved Susanoo-no-mikoto, the Shinto god of storms, from entering the dangerous Amano-Iwato caves.

People mainly ate dried chicken during the Nara period (710-794) when drying was a rudimentary way of preserving food. After Japan adopted Buddhism from China, the eating of chicken was banned for a time, as was the consumption of horse and beef, but the embargo was soon relaxed, permitting people to eat chicken, Japanese pheasant and other flying creatures again. Japanese farmers then of course began breeding more and more chickens for their own consumption. That ensured they always had plenty of eggs and didn't have to go hunting when they felt like eating a tasty, succulent chicken.

Niwatori

The generic word for chicken in Japanese is *niwatori*. This is probably a combination of the words *niwa* (garden) and *tori* (bird), which is a very plausible explanation because chickens scratched around in people's gardens. Another etymological path is based on the brown feathers most chickens have: in old Japanese, niwa meant brown. So that could also be the origin of niwatori. In the Kansai region, chickens are called *kashiwa*, because they are thought to have come from the town of Kashiwa.

Will you set the chicken, darling?

Chickens weren't only consumed; they were also used as handy alarm clocks. Since the first bunch crowed at four o'clock, the second at five and the third at six o'clock, people knew when they had to get up to go to work.

When the *toriwasa* or fighting cocks were introduced from China in the Heian period (794-1184) they also became a source of entertainment. Strangely enough, *toriwasa* is also a poetic word that means spring in the haiku culture. Given that Japanese chickens had been extensively crossed with the Japanese pheasant – a very territorial creature and moreover monogamous – they became excellent fighters as a means of protecting their territory and family from the Chinese invaders.

Chickens in the Edo period (1603-1867)

A rough distinction can be made between three varieties of chicken in Japan: firstly there are the layers (usually Mediterranean varieties, Leghorn and the native Jidori), secondly the Cochin (a huge variety that originated in China) and lastly the Shamo & Malay (Thai varieties, more commonly used as fighting cocks). The Bantam, the Silkie and the Tomaru popped up in the Edo period, having mostly arrived from the Chinese mainland. They were of course enthusiastically crossed with native Japanese varieties. Cock fights were immensely popular in this period.

The very first poulterers

Although the third *shogun* in the Edo period had already encouraged the development of chicken farms, it wasn't until the period of economic stability and affluence under the eighth shogun that chickens started to be traded. The expansion of the chicken trade took place mainly around the river Kisone, close to where Tokyo is today. Following the restoration of the Empire in 1868, this area was extended to include the prefectures of Saitama, Chiba, Ibaragi and Fukushima, all situated around Tokyo. The *shogun* in the north, Masamune Date, was allocated a variety they called Golden Polish which ensured that the economic expansion of his feudal policy was a success. In contrast, in the centre of Japan, specifically around Tokai and Nagoya, there was a proliferation of farms encouraged by the authorities where the Nagoya Cochin was bred. These Samurai farms were very prized due to their exceptionally high quality standards.

Then again, the growing population of Osaka went to the Shimane prefecture for supplies, where the Izumo Cochin and Izumo Akoku were the preferred breeds. To get the best eggs, the discerning population of Osaka liked to go to Fukuoka on Kyushu.

Try a lark for a change…

Not a lot of chicken was eaten at the beginning of the Edo period; preference was given to Japanese pheasant, goose, quail, cockerel, bulbul and lark. Eating chicken was a real sign of affluence and luxury. The end of the Edo period was accompanied by a lessening in the influence of Buddhism, which led to more meat being eaten. One example was Sukiyaki, a popular beef dish, which won instant popularity throughout the country. But even then a juicy chicken was still considered an even greater luxury. The Meiji period (1868-1912) – sometimes jokingly called the meat period – would change all that.

The first chicken kebab in Japan

The Meiji, Taisho and Showa periods spanned the years from 1868 to 1989. The reforms that took place from the Meiji-ishin on (the Japanese Revolution) were drastic, not just in a political sense. Japan became a true Empire again under the 122nd emperor of Japan, Emperor Meiji, and he gave the green light for meat to be consumed.

The popularity and high demand for chicken led to the emergence of food stalls in the streets, especially near entrances to temples, at parties or on bridges. Because chicken was so expensive, stallholders padded out the volume of those they had bought by mixing them with the last remnants of meat from carcasses they had dug out from the waste bins of expensive and exclusive chicken restaurants. This helped to keep the price down and gave them an economically marketable product. The chicken was then chopped finely, impaled on a skewer and grilled. This practice originated in the Edo period when vegetables were often cooked by sticking them on a skewer and dipping them in soup. These stalls certainly didn't just sell chicken; usually they sold beef entrails, horsemeat and dog meat too, but the name *yakitori* (literally: grilled chicken) caught on to such an extent that it has remained, even though these traders actually sold a wide range of meat.

Yakiton versus kushikatsu or east versus west

A major earthquake in Kanto in 1923 – we are now at the end of the Taisho period (1912-1926) – was followed by a proliferation of stalls selling *yakiton* (grilled pork). Their main customers were businessmen who ate it accompanied by a glass of whisky. In contrast, the popularity of *kushikatsu* – or deep-fried pork on skewers – increased in Kansai in the west of Japan. The popularity of the two dishes eventually prompted the arrival of *yakitori*.

The arrival of yakitori

Higher returns at a lower cost are an essential part of the *yakitori* economic model. Most of the native varieties of chicken in Japan, which were consumed in such numbers that they were almost extinct by 1952, were too expensive for this type of food. During the Second World War the Japanese were subject to severe rationing and the popularity of the *yakitori* stalls suffered greatly. Even in the *yakitori* restaurants, expensive chicken usually had to make way for pork and beef cooked in a sweet sauce based on soy sauce and sugar, honey or *mirin*. We still find these flavours in current methods of preparation. Once the rationing of flour was lifted in 1951, other food stalls started to become popular again, such as *tokoyaki, okonomiyaki* and the *kushikatsu*. The popularization of chicken, however, led to the yakitori kitchen becoming increasingly refined and more popular than ever.

Nowadays, needless to say, high-calibre native chicken breeds have returned again to supply the top *yakitori* restaurants in the country. These cult spots have become virtual places of pilgrimage for all chicken lovers and, despite their simple appearance, they should be on every foodie's bucket list.

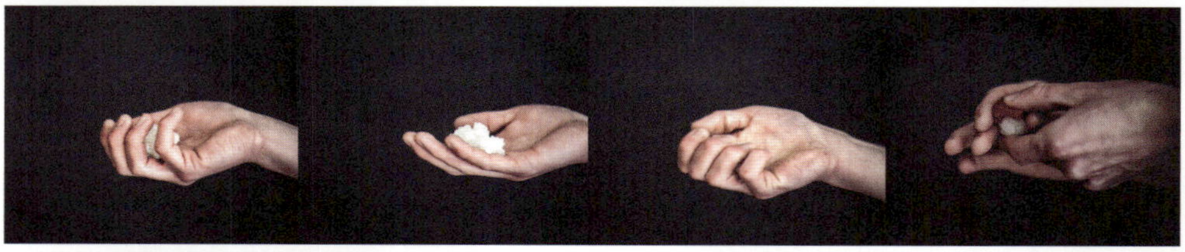

Dimitri Proost

I am the first to admit that to become a fully-qualified Japanese chef, you need to invest many, many years, a lot of time and acquire a huge amount of knowledge. A case in point is the son of Jiro Ono, who only received his father's blessing to stand on his own two feet after an apprenticeship lasting 40 years, and his chief apprentice, Nakazawa was only considered good enough to start his own restaurant in NYC after 18 years. And yet there are some young chefs who seem to be the reincarnation of an ancient Japanese soul. I feel a little like that. When I landed in Japan for the first time, I felt at home remarkably quickly, something everyone who was with me found strange. The same thing happened to Dimitri Proost, who would seem to possess much more Japanese blood and soul than you would think at first sight.

At the age of only 22, he has already worked at Hakkasan, Yamazato, Zuma and 't Fornuis: a very impressive record for such a young guy. Leaving Hakkasan and Zuma waving contacts at him, he opened Dim, a tiny restaurant seating only 16 in the historic centre of Antwerp, where with a little imagination you could conceivably be in a diminutive *izakaya* in a nameless street in Minato-ku.

Modern Japanese with a western twist is how I would describe his take on Japanese food. Sometimes it tastes as if I were in the über-hip Zuma in London and sometimes as if I were in Muromachi Wakuden, a classic bastion in Kyoto, because his food is bursting with tradition. In any case, he can make sushi like no one else and he leaves nothing to chance, which is as it should be. And in doing so, if you ask me, he is continually setting new standards for Japanese food in Belgium.

A class act with a traditional knife made from pure *tamahagane,* he creates carefully-considered, fundamental dishes with the focus and dedication of an old Japanese chef. Many colleagues of his age become caught up in current trends and cook as if everything is a competition: who can put the most on a plate or who is best at incorporating the most effects on a single plate to produce a haphazard dissonance. Dimitri's food is exactly the opposite; it is pure and his plates tell entire stories that need very few words.

With a little imagination you could conceivably be in a diminutive izakaya in a nameless street in Minato-ku.

→ Yakitori: chicken cooked in a sweet sauce of soy sauce and sugar, honey or mirin.

YAKITORI

INGREDIENTS

4 boneless chicken thighs ·
2 tsp. *shichimi togarashi* ·
4 leeks, washed and cut into chunks; ·
only use the inner, yellow parts

For the marinade
4 Tbsp. soy sauce ·
4 Tbsp. sake ·
4 Tbsp. mirin ·
1-2 Tbsp. sugar ·

METHOD

Heat up the barbecue, grill or grill pan.

Put the chicken pieces and chunks of leek on skewers.

Season with the *shichimi togarashi*.

Leave the chicken to marinate for at least two hours.

Grill the skewers.

TORIWASA

INGREDIENTS

- 200 ml mirin
- 200 ml rice vinegar
- one fresh, good quality chicken including liver, heart and stomach
- 1 white winter radish (daikon)
- kombu, approx. 4 cm
- a handful of bonito flakes
- juice of two limes
- 2 Tbsp. soy sauce
- 5 g wasabi
- 2 spring onions

METHOD

First prepare the *ponzu shoyu*. Heat the mirin and the rice vinegar for 5 minutes with a handful of bonito flakes and the kombu. Leave the liquid to cool. Mix the lime juice with the soy sauce to taste.

Grate the white radish very finely and marinate it in the ponzu shoyu.

Place the chicken in a pan of boiling, salted water for one minute. Now plunge it into ice water.

Brown the chicken a little using a kitchen blow torch or singe it on all sides in a little oil in a hot frying pan for a few seconds.

Slice it thinly, sashimi style, including the entrails.

Serve with the white radish and the wasabi.

Sprinkle finely chopped spring onion on top.

TSUKUNE

INGREDIENTS

10 shiso leaves ·
2 spring onions, finely chopped ·
500 g minced chicken ·
1 Tbsp. white miso ·
2 Tbsp. sesame oil ·

For the marinade: see the recipe for yakitori p 47.

METHOD

Chop the shiso and the spring onion very finely.

Fry ⅓ of the mince and leave to cool.

Mix the raw mince with the miso, the sesame oil, the fried mince, the shiso and the spring onion.

Coat your hands in sesame oil and make oval shapes from the mince, then prick them onto a skewer.

Grill the skewers on the barbecue or bake them in the oven.

Brush regularly with the marinade.

Coat your hands in sesame oil and form the mince into oval shapes.

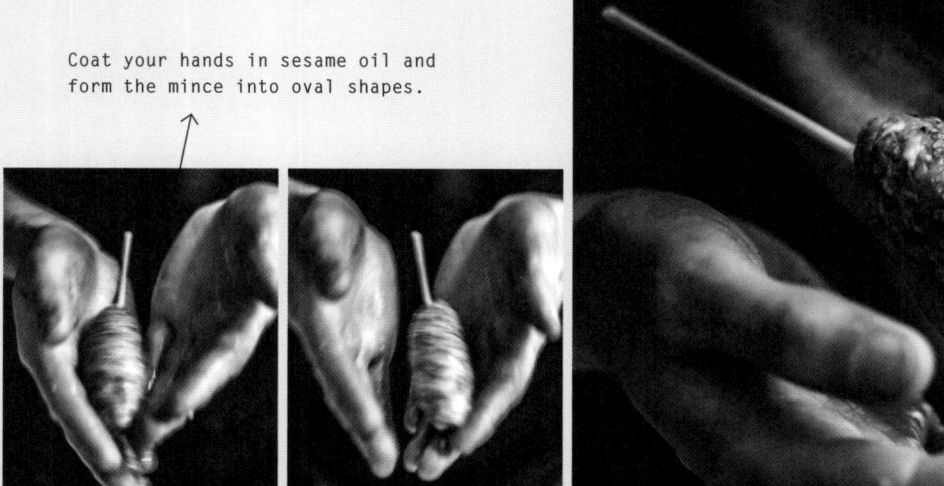

TORI NO KARAAGE

INGREDIENTS

500 g boneless chicken thighs, cut into 2.5 cm cubes

For the marinade
1 Tbsp. fresh ginger, grated
1 Tbsp. sake
2 Tbsp. soy sauce
2 cloves of garlic, chopped finely
2 tsp. granulated sugar
potato starch

oil for deep-frying
lemon juice
salt

METHOD

Make the marinade by mixing together the sake, ginger, soy sauce, garlic and sugar.

Marinate the chicken pieces for at least an hour.

Pat the chicken pieces dry then dredge them in the potato starch and fry them in hot oil.

Season to taste with lemon juice and salt.

MIZUTAKI

INGREDIENTS

- 1 litre dashi stock
- 3 boneless chicken thighs
- optional: a piece of white fish and some crustaceans
- 50 g tofu
- 1 spring onion, finely chopped
- a couple of shiitake, sliced
- 1 onion, shredded
- 1/4 Chinese cabbage, washed and cut into strips
- 1 carrot, sliced
- 1 carton of enoki mushrooms, wiped and with roots removed
- 20 g spinach leaves

For the *sukiyaki* sauce
- 200 ml mirin
- 100 ml sake
- 200 ml soy sauce
- 80 g sugar

METHOD

Heat the dashi stock with some of the *sukiyaki* sauce.

Cut the ingredients into similar sizes so that they will cook at about the same rate.

Boil all the ingredients in the stock, in order of cooking time – i.e. the chicken first and the spinach last – so that all the ingredients are cooked properly.

TSUBU-MISO GAKO HINADORI NO OVEN YAKI

INGREDIENTS

1 spring chicken ·
1 Saikyo Tsuke Doko miso ·
1 sheet of cedar wood paper ·
1 Tbsp. toasted sesame seeds ·

METHOD

Marinate the spring chicken in the miso for 24 hours.

Pre-heated the oven to 200 °C. Place the chicken on the cedar wood and roast it in the oven for eight minutes.

Sprinkle with toasted sesame seeds.

SOBORO DON

INGREDIENTS

- 100 g Japanese rice
- sushi vinegar
- 500 g minced chicken
- 2 spring onions, finely chopped
- 1 Tbsp. fresh ginger, chopped very finely
- 1 Tbsp. mirin
- 1 Tbsp. sake
- 2 Tbsp. soy sauce
- 2 eggs
- 2 Tbsp. sugar
- 1 small onion, shredded

METHOD

Boil the rice until tender and season to taste with sushi vinegar.

Fry the minced chicken in the pan, breaking it up as it fries.

Add the shredded onion and ginger.

Sprinkle with mirin and saki.

Stir the minced chicken to break it up into small pieces.

Add the soy sauce.

Beat the eggs with the sugar and make an omelette.

While the eggs are cooking, break them up as in scrambled egg.

Place a layer of rice in the bottom of a bowl then cover half of it with chicken, place the egg next to it and the spring onion in the middle.

WANG RONG CHICK CHICK...

There is nothing that makes us more aware of cultural differences than when something appears on a global medium that seems to make no sense at all to a large part of the world. That happened not so long ago with the video clip of the Chinese artist Wang Rong performing *Chick Chick*. The clip, which is full of Chinese symbolism, went viral with over 50 million hits. It contains plenty of social criticism as well as entertainment but the average westerner was left with nothing but puzzlement. It's a tune that's difficult to get out of your head, with lyrics in a language invented by the artist that animals can use to communicate with each other, including *'chicken cluck click day, little chick cluck cluck day'* and *'rooster whoa whoa whoa'*. The clip and its success fascinated international newspapers such as *The Daily Telegraph* in the USA and *The Mirror* in Beijing.

Darwin versus Smithsonian
The last word about the domestication of chickens has not been uttered. Darwin was convinced that the first farmyard chickens appeared in the Indus valley (present-day Pakistan), but the prestigious Smithsonian places them earlier in northern China. The discovery of bones there led to estimates that the Chinese were already keeping chickens some 10,000 years ago.

Given the enormous size of the country and the vast diversity of its cookery, it is incredibly interesting for devotees of chickens. By and large, there are four major schools. The first is Shandong that includes the illustrious, refined aristocratic cuisine from Beijing. The famous Shanghai style of cookery can be classified as Yang, while the most well-known, Cantonese, Hakka Hong Kong and Macau are in the style of Yue/Guandong. And finally, there is the renowned Hunan cuisine from Sichuan.

A dragon with chicken's feet
Chinese culture attaches great importance to symbolism, and that applies to food too. The chicken is no exception, in that it symbolises both the dragon and the phoenix. At a Chinese wedding, chicken's feet, sometimes referred to as phoenix feet, are often served with other dragon symbols such as lobster. Chicken is also very popular at Chinese New Year. When chicken is served

→ Leung Kwai Lam, or Tai Lo for friends. This highly gifted chef is truly exceptional, conjuring up one masterly dish after another with apparent serenity.

whole it symbolises unity within a family. Chicken served with its tail, feet and head symbolises togetherness and the coming together of families. This is also reflected in the sign of the cockerel, one of the 12 signs in the Chinese horoscope. Here, the cockerel is a symbol of honesty and of physical and moral strength; since it tends towards the yang side, it signifies happiness, loyalty and protection.

A white phoenix with black bones

Traditional Chinese medicine and the medicinal cookery associated with it involve eating things that prevent medical problems rather than cure them. It is not unusual for people who go to these restaurants to have a consultation with a traditional Chinese Qi Gong doctor before eating, who will examine their energy channels and decide what their body requires at that moment to restore balance. This traditional approach makes a clear distinction between meat from chickens and meat from cockerels. Chicken is yang and is mainly recommended for middle-aged men, but is strongly advised against if the patient has skin problems and general rashes. Meat from cockerels is naturally yin and because it makes people strong, it is mainly recommended for older people, women and especially women in the last weeks of pregnancy. The ultimate chicken for medicinal cookery is the 'chicken with black bones' or the *wu gu ji,* also known as the 'white phoenix' *(bai feng).* Strangely enough, this chicken has white feathers and almost black flesh and bones.

The diversity and originality Chinese chefs apply to chicken is almost endless. There is only one man in Belgium (and therefore only one restaurant), who comes close to emulating the authenticity and versatility of the top Chinese kitchens and that is Leung Kwai Lam, or Tai Lo for friends. This highly gifted chef is truly exceptional, conjuring up one masterly dish after another with apparent serenity. His repertoire and in-depth knowledge reveal an inordinately long period spent studying Chinese cookery and its medicinal uses. He is the type of Chinese chef who is in total control and he reminds me in some way of Mr Chu, the central figure in Ang Lee's magnificent film, *Eat drink man woman*. Not just because of the evident mastery he displays, but also because of the gratifying effect this food has on the human organism. *Eat drink man woman* is an apt quote from Confucius' Book of Rites, which states that everything a man desires can be found in sexual pleasure, food and drink.

Leung Kwai Lam works his magic every day in his modest restaurant, 5 Flavors Mmei in hip South Antwerp and he can count on a multitude of true fans who come to his restaurant as if they were undertaking a pilgrimage to a Chinese temple of food. Whatever you do, don't miss the Dim Sum here: this is where you'll find the quintessential Dim Sum and it will not fail to impress.

BO BO CHICKEN

INGREDIENTS

2 boneless chicken legs *(approx. 570 g)*, cut into 2 x 3-cm pieces
1 tsp. light soy sauce
2 tsp. potato starch
5 Tbsp. water
2 Tbsp. oil
2 g ginger, julienned
2 g garlic, brunoised
1 spring onion, julienned
1 chili pepper, chopped
5 star anise
1 Tbsp. Shaoxing wine
1 Tbsp. Chinkiang black rice vinegar
1 tsp dark soy sauce
1.5 Tbsp. sugar

METHOD

Marinate the chicken legs for at least 30 minutes in the light soy sauce and 1 teaspoon of sugar.

Fry the chicken legs until they are almost cooked through.

Heat a wok to 100 °C; pour in the oil, then add the ginger, garlic, spring onion, chili pepper and star anise; fry for about 10 seconds. Now add the chicken followed by the light and dark soy sauce.

Add the Shaoxing and the Chingkiang, simmer until cooked, stirring continuously.

Add the water, sugar and 1 teaspoon of diluted potato starch and simmer on a gentle heat until it begins to caramelise.

STUFFED CHICKEN

INGREDIENTS

1 free-range chicken weighing at least 1.2 kg ·
300 g large prawns ·
3 Tbsp. water ·
1 tsp. salt ·
2 tsp. sugar ·
1/3 tsp. ground white pepper ·
2 Tbsp. potato starch ·
10 g lemongrass, only the white part, very finely chopped ·
50 g spring onion, finely chopped ·
50 g celery, finely chopped ·
1 litre oil ·

For the skin
1 Tbsp. molasses ·
2 Tbsp. red wine vinegar ·
350 ml water ·

METHOD

Make an incision into the chicken along each breast, being careful not to break the skin. Remove the chicken carcass but leave the drumstick and wing joints attached to the skin.

Mix the meat from the chicken with the large prawns then chop the mixture as finely as possible until it resembles minced meat.

Add the water and one teaspoon of salt and mix very thoroughly. Now add the sugar, the white pepper and the potato starch. Follow that with the lemongrass, celery and the spring onion.

Cover and put the mixture in the fridge.

For the skin
Mix the first two ingredients and heat to a temperature of 80 °C until everything has melted. Spread the skin out as much as possible and pull it tight using chopsticks.

Boil 350 ml water and pour it over the outer side of the skin; now paint the skin with the melted ingredients.

Leave the skin stretched out in a dry, preferably windy place (a ventilator will do the trick) for eight hours to dry.

To finish
Remove the minced meat from the fridge.

Remove the wings and the drumsticks from the skin using scissors or a knife.

Spread the minced meat over the inner side of the skin (now stiff) and press it down firmly by only pressing on this inner side.

Heat 1 litre of oil to 120-130 °C and fry the chicken wings and drumsticks. Fry the minced meat on the skin for about 10 minutes, until the meat is cooked.

Remove everything from the pan and drain.

Reheat the oil to 180 °C then replace all the meat and fry until it is golden.

Cut into pieces and reform into the shape of a chicken.

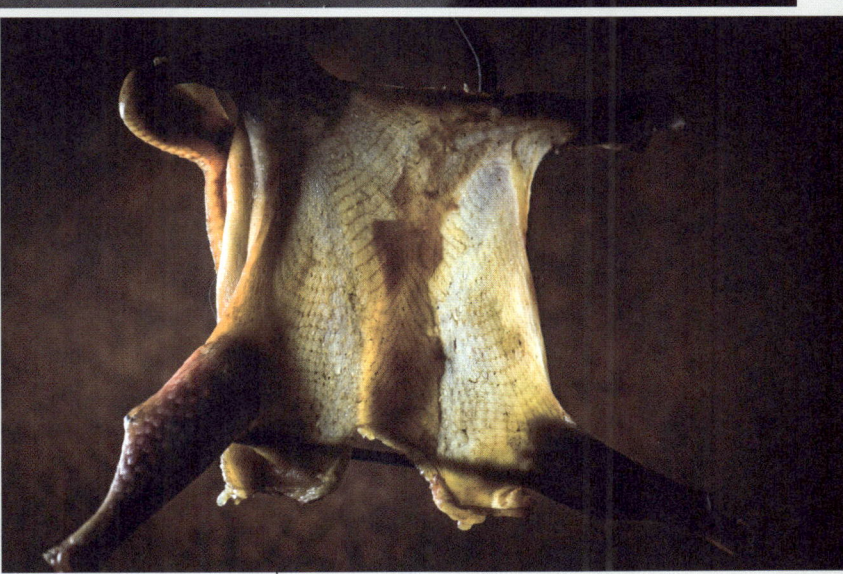

Leave the skin stretched out in a dry, preferably windy place (a ventilator will do the trick) for eight hours to dry.

THAI-STYLE CHICKEN LEGS

INGREDIENTS

For the sauce

- 1 blade of lemongrass, very finely chopped
- 1 Tbsp. white vinegar
- 0.5 tsp. ground white pepper
- 1 cucumber, julienned
- juice of five limes
- 50 g spring onion, julienned
- 2 Tbsp. fish sauce
- 5-10 g fresh coriander, chopped
- pinch of salt
- 5 Tbsp. sugar
- 10 very small hot red chili peppers

For the meat

- 10 white chicken legs

METHOD

Sauce

Mix all the ingredients together – except the chicken legs. Taste and correct seasoning, then place in the fridge.

The chicken legs

Place the chicken legs in boiling water for 18 minutes; remove them and cool them immediately by plunging them into a bowl of ice water

Debone the chicken legs; plunge the boned chicken legs back in the ice water for 5 minutes.

Pat the chicken legs dry and place them in the sauce; mix carefully and leave for half an hour before serving.

XIAO LUNG PAO

INGREDIENTS

For the filling
1 spring onion, finely chopped ·
2 chicken breasts, chopped into small pieces ·
1 litre chicken stock ·
100 g Chinese mushrooms ·
5 prawns (size 16-20), chopped ·
2 scallops, chopped ·
1 tsp. sesame oil ·
2 tsp. potato starch ·
2 tsp. sugar ·
1 tsp. salt ·
pinch of white pepper ·

For the pancakes
20 g plain flour ·
0.5 tsp. baking powder ·
570 g high gluten flour ·
9 eggs ·

METHOD

For the filling

Mix all the ingredients thoroughly, except for the stock, and place in the fridge.

For the pancakes

Thoroughly mix all the ingredients for at least 10 minutes and knead them into a ball.

Separate into small balls as big as you like, between 30 and 100 grams each, then roll them out to form little pancakes.

To finish

Place the filling on the pancakes and form them into xiao lung pao.

Heat some chicken stock to about 90 °C. Add salt and pepper to taste. Cook the dumplings; a 50 g dumpling will take about 20 minutes.

Place the dumplings in soup bowls and pour some chicken stock over them.

LITTLE CHICKEN CURRY DUMPLINGS

INGREDIENTS

For the filling
- 2 Tbsp. oil
- 1 piece of lemongrass (just the white part), very finely chopped
- 20 g onion, very finely chopped
- 10 g garlic, very finely chopped
- 3 curry leaves, very finely chopped
- 2 tsp. Malaysian curry powder
- 3 Tbsp. Shaoxing wine
- 570 g chicken breast, finely chopped
- 20 cl coconut milk
- 3 tsp. sugar
- 1 tsp. salt
- 3 Tbsp. potato starch

For the dough
- 57 cl water
- 620 g Tang flour
- 90 g potato starch

METHOD

The dough

Boil the water and then turn off the heat. Mix 570 grams of Tang flour with 40 grams of potato starch in a pan then add the boiled water a little at a time. Keep stirring. Mix in the rest of the Tang flour and potato starch, knead and form a ball. Cover with a damp cloth.

The filling

Heat the wok and pour in the oil. Add the lemongrass, onion, garlic, curry leaves and curry powder; add the Shaoxing wine five seconds later.

Add the chicken, together with the coconut milk, the sugar and the salt. Simmer on a medium heat until everything is cooked; about eight minutes.

Mix the potato starch with a little water and pour slowly into the wok, stirring all the time, to bind.

To finish

Let the filling cool completely on a dish.

Make little balls from the dough and roll them out to form a sort of pancake.

Pour the filling onto the pancakes and form little packages, for example ha kau or triangles.

Steam them for a few minutes to cook them.

STUFFED STEAMED BAMBOO FUNGI

INGREDIENTS

- 100 g dried bamboo fungi
- 28 g dried fat choy (black moss)
- 570 g chicken breast, cut into 3 x 1.5-cm pieces
- 1 tsp. salt
- 2 tsp. sugar
- pinch of ground white pepper
- 1 tsp. sesame oil
- 1 tsp. potato starch
- 2 Tbsp. oyster sauce
- 3 Tbsp. Shaoxing wine

METHOD

Put the bamboo fungi and the fat choy in separate bowls and pour boiling water over them; leave for 3 hours.

Marinate the pieces of chicken in a mixture of salt, sugar, white pepper, Shaoxing wine and sesame oil and then add 1 teaspoon of potato starch. Mix well and place in the fridge for 3 hours.

After 3 hours, squeeze out the bamboo fungi and the fat choy.

Remove the chicken from the marinade then wrap the pieces of chicken in the bamboo fungi. Place the fat choy on top.

Steam for 12 minutes.

Heat the oyster sauce and pour over the fungi.

Korea's national dish is kimchee. ←

JINJUU BEFORE SWINE

Korea, or Uri-nara as it is called in Korea, is a country with a very rich gastronomic culture. Incidentally, the western name Korea is an exonym of Goryeo, the 10th-century dynasty. The Dutchman, Hendrick Hamel (1630-1692), a shipwrecked sailor who lived in Korea for 13 years, introduced the name and spelling of Korea. Koreans who live in the south call their country Hanguk; South Koreans use Bukhan when they are talking about North Korea, while North Koreans call their country Joseon. They both use Uri Nara, which means 'our country'.

Gastronomically, Korea is a country with a lot to offer, but there are still very few Korean restaurants worth their name in the west. If you do come across one, it's usually a bland, watered-down version of *gogigui,* or Korean barbecue. And that's a shame, because ignorance breeds contempt. That makes it all the more unusual for such a rich, ancient gastronomic culture to be conquering the world with a very simple chicken dish, *yangnyeom*. Korea's gastronomic culture reflects its philosophy of life. Pursuit of a balance between ying and yang: hot, cold, mild and spicy... An explosion of flavours, smells and textures: culinary sensations in which simplicity is the main ingredient.

Korean cuisine is becoming known due to a number of indefatigable international ambassadors, and I'd like to turn the spotlight on one of them: Judy Joo, who is based in London. Korean cuisine could not have a better ambassador than Judy Joo. She presents a number of TV cooking programmes in the UK and the US that highlight Korean dishes. Her enthusiasm for her country's food is infectious.

She is a true *jinjuu,* Korean for pearl and the name of her first restaurant in London, where she unleashes her contemporary vision of traditional Korean food on the critical London public. She does what she loves on two floors in the trendy district around Carnaby Street. The ground floor is given over to *anju,* titbits you eat while having a drink. The fantastic Korean fried chicken or *yangnyeom* steals the show here, as do the Bulgogi style burgers and the delicious

♥ KOREAN ♥ ★ FRIED ★ CHICKEN!

savoury dumplings, while downstairs a more sophisticated experience awaits.

Chicken Gangnam style

Korean fried chicken or *yangnyeom* is already a hit in cities like London, NYC and Berlin and now looks as if it is heading to be a buzz word in hip parts of Paris and Belgian cities too. The trick with Korean fried chicken is that it is fried twice, the way the Belgians fry their world-famous fries. Maximum crispness guaranteed.

Who exactly was the first to invent the now world-renowned delicacy *yangnyeom tongdak* is currently being disputed. Two restaurants have competing claims for the patent: Pelicana Chicken and Mexicana Chicken. The Pelicana certainly introduced the *yangnyeom tongdak* before its competitor, but both use strawberry jam and *gochujang* as flavourings.

A full plate of fried chicken is a truly iconic dish for South Koreans, who wash it down liberally with beer or *soju*. For the older generation, eating chicken is quite an occasion because in the period in which chicken and other meat was scarce, chicken only appeared on the table for special celebrations. There wasn't any fried chicken at all in Korea in the 1950s and 1960s: chicken was traditionally boiled with rice and ginseng, to make a dish known as *samgyetang*.

At the end of the 1960s, a restaurant called Yeongyang opened in what was then a modern shopping mall in Myeondong in the centre of Seoul. What made it noteworthy was that its kitchen was fitted with an electric oven. The crispy, yet succulent chicken bites is produced became all the rage in Korea in the 1970s and resulted in an incredible increase in the breeding of chickens and the manufacture of oils for deep-frying.

Not Kentucky fried chicken but Korean fried chicken

The first Korean fried chicken outlet opened in the Shinsegae Department Store in 1977. It took until 1984 before Kentucky fried chicken arrived here. Pelicana chicken started in 1982 with the now famous *yangnyeom,* super-crispy pieces of chicken coated in a spicy sweet sauce.

What makes Korean fried chicken so different to ours, say, or the American variant? In Korea, chicken is fried at least twice and sometimes three times, which makes it even crispier, and then it is coated in a variety of flavourings to make it richer.

Korea's national dish is and remains *kimchee* of course. When Koreans are urged to smile for a photo, they even say '*kimchee*' (where we say 'cheese'). *Kimchee* is superior to Korean fried chicken because it is one of the oldest recipes, and it consists of preserved, fermented and pickled vegetables. References to it can even be found in the 7th-century Xin Nan Shan poems. There are 187 officially recognised varieties of *kimchee,* but needless to say, in practice there are as many *kimchee* recipes as there are people who make *kimchee*.

KOREAN DOUBLE FRIED CHICKEN

INGREDIENTS

- 1 small yellow onion, roughly grated
- 2 cloves of garlic, finely chopped
- 1/2 tsp. salt
- 1/4 tsp. of black pepper
- 10 boneless chicken thighs
- 2.5 tsp. gojuchang (Korean chili paste)
- 2.5 tsp. tomato ketchup
- 50 g sugar
- 1.5 tsp. roasted sesame seeds
- juice of half a lemon
- oil for frying
- 75 g plain flour
- 80 g cornflour
- chili paste
- sesame seeds

METHOD

Mix the onion, garlic, salt and pepper in a large bowl. Add the pieces of chicken and mix everything together. Cover the bowl and leave to marinate for at least an hour.

Mix the chili paste, tomato ketchup, sugar, sesame seeds and lemon juice in a large bowl. Check the seasoning for balance.

Pour the oil into a deep fat fryer or heavy pan and heat to 170 °C. Mix the cornflour with the plain flour and season with salt and pepper.

Fry small batches at a time! Remove the chicken from the marinade, dredge with the flour mixture and drop them gently into the hot oil. Fry them for 3-4 minutes then remove and drain; continue until all the pieces of chicken have been fried.

Now heat the oil to 190 °C and fry the chicken again, in batches, for another 3-4 minutes.

Place the chicken pieces on kitchen paper to drain off the excess fat then, while the chicken is still hot, brush it with chili paste and sprinkle with sesame seeds.

MANDELBROT

Trying to explain Indian cuisine is about as easy as explaining chaos theory. Throughout more than 5000 years of history, India has had to accept an extraordinary number of ethnic groups and conquerors, all of whom influenced the country in countless ways.

To understand and get to the bottom of the evolution of India's native cuisine, you first of all have to realise that this country is anything but homogenous. The local differences that make it so fascinating are in many cases due to all its different regions and religions. In a country with over a billion inhabitants and almost all climates, the diversity of the food is as diverse as the population itself.

Hinduism and Islam are the two dominant religions that have exerted the most influence on the customs surrounding food, the methods used and its diversity. Each wave of migration brought new influences too. The vegetarianism typical of Hindus is very widespread, while Muslim traditions have influenced and shaped the preparation of meat in particular. The Portuguese, Persians and the British also introduced their own significant influence on the country's food and gastronomy. The British for instance were the ones to bring in tea.

Tandoori vs tikka

Tandoori chicken is in my opinion by far the best and most intriguing way of cooking chicken that there is. The smell, the appearance and naturally the taste cannot be compared with any other chicken recipe I know. *Tandoori murgh* or tandoori chicken is inextricably associated with India, but actually this complex, aromatic explosion has its origins elsewhere. It is a dish that originated during the Persian Mughal Empire that ruled northern India somewhere between 1526 and 1757. The rulers were direct descendants of Genghis Khan. The impact this empire had was enormous; even then, about 150 million people lived in within its boundaries. Its principal cuisine, Mughlai, was significantly influenced by Iran, Kashmir and Punjab. Tandoori chicken became popular especially among the Muslim population when the Mughal Empire fell apart.

The dish found its way to the hearts of the people in northern India and Pakistan and also to mine. Incisions are made in a chicken thigh before it is marinated in yogurt, lime or lemon juice and a mixture of fresh herbs and spices. After being cooked in a tandoori oven, it is transformed into a bundle of emotions. The yogurt and lemon or lime juice makes the chicken very soft. A short blast of heat in a traditional, very hot (500-600 °C) tandoori is enough to work its magic to produce a fiery-red chicken thigh that will change your idea of chicken for ever.

The difference between *tikka* and *tandoori* is that tandoori only uses pieces of chicken containing a bone such as the thigh or drumstick, while tikka only uses deboned or breast pieces.

Just a footnote: although the British had an enormous impact on Indian cookery and gastronomy there has recently been a movement in the other direction. After India became independent in 1948, it took less than 40 years for the most popular dish in the United Kingdom to become... *chicken tikka masala!*

My kingdom for a samosa

Weak at the knees, I rang the bell at the entrance to the lion's den. I was about to meet my future mother-in-law and I was now regretting my idea of making *samosa* for her as a present – however brilliant it had seemed at the outset. How hard can it be?

Every northern Indian woman can do it, so... I decided to switch roles for once. I was bringing my own home-made samosa for this northern Indian woman, in whose kitchen I was now standing. The samosa was accepted and immediately heated up in a hot oven. Full of curiosity, she bit into it and when I saw a radiant smile appear on her face, my tension started to ebb away. Mission accomplished!

I am eternally grateful to Shirani Gunasekara from Colombo and Mahli Shahbaz from Lahore. I regularly ate samosa in their simple, yet elegant restaurant and I became addicted to this triangular taste sensation. I got hold of their recipe for the filling by exerting all my natural charms on them.

Samosa is a very popular snack/lunch in northern India and Pakistan and by extension the entire Arabic-speaking world: Turkey, Goa, Portugal... The word samosa comes from the Persian word *sanbosag* and the first references to it appeared in the 10th century. The Iranian historian, Abolfazl Bayhaqi (995-1075) mentioned them in his writings and by the 13th-14th centuries, samosa had become widespread in the wake of the expeditions by Arab traders.

Samosa have been written about regularly throughout history, and mostly praised highly. Amir Khusro, a poet at the court of the sultan of Delhi, described the ingredients in one of his poems: he talked about meat, *ghee,* onions, almonds and spices. A recipe for *qutab,* which Hindus call *sanbusah,* can be found in the *Ain-i-Akbari,* an important Mughal gastronomic document of cultural heritage written in the 16th century.

If the filling for this triangular delicacy does not consist of *aloo matar* (a vegetarian stew consisting of potato, peas, onion, ghee and a balanced mixture of spices) it is usually made of chicken: minced chicken with a balanced mixture of spices. The sauce is usually yogurt with cumin and spices, which provides a cooling contrast to the hot spiciness of the filling.

Making the triangular shape is something you need to practise a few times to become really skilled, but it isn't too difficult once you have mastered the technique. It can be made from puff pastry, filo pastry or special samosa pastry. Ghee is often confused with clarified butter but it is actually quite different. Frying the samosa in ghee is ideal as it gives it an even richer flavour.

Chicken 65 or 78 or 82

Chicken 65 is a mythical dish that has only been around for a short time. A.M. Buhari, the owner of the Buhari Hotel in Chennai invented a chicken dish in 1965 and he gave it the rather uninspiring name of Chicken 65. It is a pretty spicy dish, even by Indian standards. Buhari has kept the exact recipe secret but it is assumed that, apart from the fact that the dish was created in 1965, there could be 65 chili peppers in it. Moreover, the chicken is slaughtered at 65 days old, so it is in fact a *poussin*.

As well as that, Buhari created a Chicken 78, a Chicken 82 and a Chicken 90, each called after their respective creation dates. It is the most recent dish to have acquired a sort of cult status, following in the footsteps of old traditional classics like butter chicken and *panu puri*. Although it hasn't yet reached any gastronomic encyclopaedia, influential magazines have attributed it as his invention. It appeared in all its glory in The Hindu in 2013 and it was one of the questions in Siddarth Basu's well-known TV quiz show.

Chickens seem to have been a permanent feature in India and were always popular in both daily meals and celebrations. Perhaps they really have been around for ever because some genetic studies point to the Indian sub-continent as one of the possible cradles of chicken. What we do know is that the domesticated chicken was exported to Lydia (former West Anatolia) from India and from there it conquered Greece and then Egypt. According to the writings of Thoetmoses III, the 'bird that gives birth every day' came to Egypt from the country between Syria and Shinar and Babylon.

The chicken varieties that are now the most popular in India are Asil or Aseel in the north, Brahma, Giriraja, Gramapriya, Kadaknath, Kuroiler and Vanaraja. Most are direct descendants of the primordial varieties.

Shirkhan is a tribute to Mumbai street food. This is where you'll find the real flavours of Indian food.

De met mozaïek belegde blinkende tandoorioven spuwt verse naan en fantastische tikka.

Hari is a true master in flavours and extractives and knows better than anyone how to present the real sense of India.

Hariprasad Shetty

It isn't that easy to find an Indian chef in our region who truly understands the complexity of Indian food. Most Indian restaurants offer no more than bland spin-offs of this high-class gastronomic culture. Hariprasad (or Hari to his friends) is however one of these rare creatures. Hari cannot deny his Indian roots, nor would he want to, although the outside world mainly sees him excelling in flashy Asian, especially Japanese, fusion. He became famous as a chef at Nobu London, a restaurant that specialises in Nikkei cuisine and has occupied the top slot in the list of places to be in London and elsewhere in the world. London is of course the outstanding example of a cultural melting pot and an Indian chef who cooks in a hip Japanese-Peruvian restaurant is as unusual there as here. But his heart still lies with Indian cuisine and I believe that his many years of practice in Japanese subtlety have taught him how to take his Indian cuisine to the next level.

Hari has joined the Entourage Group in Amsterdam where he works as an executive chef. He is in charge of Momo, Izakaya, The Butcher and Shirkhan. Shirkhan is the latest brainchild of owner Yossi Eliyahoo and Hari. It is a tribute to Mumbai street food. This is where you'll find the real flavours, the real style and the true nature of heart-warming Indian food. The shining tandoori oven inlaid with mosaic forms the centrepiece and the fresh naan and tikka it discharges is beyond being fantastic. De Hallen in Amsterdam can rejoice in the arrival of Shirkhan. Hari is a true master in flavours and extractives and knows better than anyone how to present the real sense of India. A master...

TANDOORI CHICKEN

INGREDIENTS

1 whole chicken ·
2 tsp. Kashmiri red chilli powder ·
3 Tbsp. lemon juice ·
salt to taste ·
1 cup thick yogurt ·
2 Tbsp. ginger paste ·
2 Tbsp. garlic paste ·
1/2 tsp garam masala powder ·
2 Tbsp. olive oil to baste ·
1/2 tsp. chaat masala ·

METHOD

Make incisions with a sharp knife on the chicken breast, legs and thighs.

Rub a mixture of one teaspoon of Kashmiri red chilli powder, one tablespoon of lemon juice and salt over the chicken and set aside for half an hour.

For the marinade, tie up yogurt in a piece of muslin and hang over a bowl for 15 to 20 minutes.

Transfer the thick yogurt into a bowl. Add the remaining Kashmiri red chilli powder, salt, ginger paste, garlic paste, the remaining lemon juice, garam masala powder and two tablespoons of olive oil.

Rub this mixture over the chicken and marinate for three to four hours in a refrigerator.

Thread the chicken onto a skewer and cook in a moderately hot tandoor (clay oven) or in a preheated oven at 200°C/400°F/Gas Mark 6 for ten to twelve minutes, or until almost done.

Baste the chicken with a little oil and cook for another four minutes. Remove and set aside.

Sprinkle on chaat masala powder and serve with onion rings and lemon wedges.

The yogurt and lemon or lime juice has the effect of making the chicken very tender. A short blast of heat in a traditional, very hot tandoori is enough for it to work its magic to produce a fiery-red chicken thigh.

CHICKEN SAAG

INGREDIENTS

- 1 kg skinless chicken cubed
- 4 Tbsp. oil
- 250 grams spinach, washed & chopped
- 100 ml water
- 3 Tbsp. oil
- 4 cm fresh ginger, minced
- 5 fresh garlic, minced
- 2 large white onions (minced or extremely finely chopped)
- 400 grams tomatoes, blanched and chopped
- 1/2 tsp. salt
- 1/2 tsp. cayenne pepper
- 1 tsp. coriander powder
- 1/2 tsp. turmeric powder
- 2 cloves
- 2 big cardamom
- 1 Tbsp. water
- 1 tsp. garam masala

METHOD

Fry the chicken in 4 tablespoons of oil for around 3 or 4 minutes until lightly browned; set aside.

Put the spinach in a pot, add 60 ml of water.

Bring to the boil and remove from heat.

When cool, grind very thoroughly (almost to a paste) in a blender and set aside.

Heat the remaining 3 tablespoons of oil in a pan and add the ginger, garlic and onions.

Fry until lightly brown.

Add tomatoes, salt, cayenne pepper, ground coriander, turmeric, cloves and cardamom.

Sprinkle with 1 Tbsp. water.

Cook for 10 minutes on a low heat.

Add chicken and milk to the pan.

Simmer until the chicken is tender (about 10 minutes).

Add spinach and garam masala to the pan.

Cook until the spinach starts sticking to the pan (about 15 minutes).

Remove from heat, add butter and cover until ready to serve with rice.

CHANA AUR KHATTE PYAAZ KA MURGH

INGREDIENTS

- 500 g chicken
- 10 Tbsp. ginger garlic paste
- salt to taste
- juice of 2 lemons
- 1.5 Tbsp. coriander powder
- 1.5 Tbsp. cumin powder
- 1 Tbsp. red chilli powder
- 1 Tbsp. chaat masala
- 1 Tbsp. anardana powder
- 1 Tbsp. garam masala powder
- 1 Tbsp. yellow chilli powder
- 1 cup chickpeas (chana)
- 1 bay leaf
- 1 Tbsp. turmeric powder
- 250 ml ghee
- 125 ml oil
- 1.5 Tbsp. cumin seeds
- 200 g onions, chopped
- 1.5 Tbsp. whole garam masala
- 150 g tomatoes
- 40 g ginger, chopped
- 6-8 green chillies
- 175 ml yogurt
- 1 bunch mint
- 125 ml fresh cream
- 4 Tbsp. pickled onions *(for garnish)*

METHOD

Marinate the chicken pieces in ginger-garlic paste as required, salt, lemon juice and dry spices.

Boil the chickpeas with the bay leaf and turmeric powder. Once the chickpeas are cooked, cool them in a bowl.

Take a pan and add ghee, marinated chicken and cook it for some time until it is golden brown.

Pour oil into a separate pan and heat. Now add the cumin seeds, onions and whole garam masala.

Once the onions are golden add the remaining ginger-garlic paste.

Add the tomatoes and cook for a while. Now add the chana and cook for 10 minutes.

Once it is done, grind the onion and tomato masala into a paste with ginger and green chillies and pass through a sieve.

Add some yogurt and mint and cook again for a while. Finish by adding the chicken and the cream.

Garnish with sliced pickle onions.

GARLIC NAAN

INGREDIENTS

400 g refined flour *(maida)* ·
25 g garlic, peeled ·
1 tsp. baking powder ·
1/2 teaspoon bicarbonate of soda ·
salt to taste ·
2 tsp. sugar ·
375 ml milk ·
2 Tbsp. yogurt ·
2 Tbsp. fresh coriander leaves, chopped ·
2 Tbsp. olive oil ·
6 Tbsp. butter ·

METHOD

Sieve the flour, leaving some aside for dusting, with the baking powder, bicarbonate of soda and salt. Grind 20 garlic cloves to a fine paste.

Chop the remaining garlic finely. Add sugar, milk, garlic paste, yogurt, chopped garlic, chopped coriander leaves to the flour mixture and mix. Add water as required and knead to form a medium soft dough.

Apply a little oil, cover with a damp cloth and set aside for at least an hour.

Punch the dough with your hands to make it soft and pliable

Divide the dough into 12 to 16 equal portions, cover and let it rest for another hour. Melt the butter.

Flatten each dough ball between your palms, apply melted butter and dust with flour.

Roll them into balls again and keep them covered for fifteen minutes. Preheat the oven to 250°C.

Roll each dough ball on a floured surface into a five to six-inch diameter disc.

Pull it from one end to get the elongated shape of a naan.

Cook in the preheated oven at 250°C for seven minutes.

You can also cook them in a tandoor till brown spots appear on the surface. Remove and serve hot drizzled with melted butter.

CHICKEN TIKKA AND NAAN WRAP WITH MINT CHUTNEY

INGREDIENTS

400 g boneless chicken thighs cut into 1/2 inch pieces ·
1 tsp. red chilli paste ·
salt to taste ·
1 tsp. ginger-garlic paste ·
4 Tbsp. thick yogurt ·
1/2 tsp. garam masala powder ·
1 lemon ·

Mint Chutney

10 g garlic ·
2 cups of torn mint leaves ·
1 Tbsp. olive oil ·
1/2 tsp. black salt *(kala namak)* ·
10 g ginger, roughly chopped ·
2 green chillies, roughly chopped ·
375 ml yogurt, whisked ·
1 Tbsp. lemon juice ·
salt to taste ·

METHOD

Marinate the chicken pieces in a mixture of red chilli paste, salt, ginger-garlic paste, yogurt, garam masala powder and lemon juice. Add 2 tablespoons of extra virgin olive oil and mix and marinate for a few hours in the refrigerator.

Put the marinated chicken on to metal skewers and cook for 25 minutes in a pre-heated Tandoor or an oven heated to 250 °C.

Turn the skewers so that the chicken gets cooked evenly all around.

Mint chutney

Heat the oil in a pan, add garlic and sauté. Sprinkle on black salt and sauté till well browned.

Put the mint leaves into a mixer. Add the ginger and green chillies. Add the sautéed garlic. Add two tablespoons of water with salt and grind to a fine paste.

Add the paste to the yogurt and mix well. Add the lemon juice and salt and mix. Pass this mixture through a muslin cloth, squeezing well to get a smooth chutney.

Wrap

Place the garlic naan on a chopping board. Spread some mint chutney over it. Add freshly sliced red onion (washed). Add Chicken Tikka Pieces. And roll it tight.

MURG DO PYAAZA

INGREDIENTS

1 kg chicken (1 inch pieces on the bone) ·
25 almonds, roasted ·
1 Tbsp. sunflower seeds *(chironji)* ·
1 Tbsp. poppy seeds *(khuskhus)* ·
125 ml oil ·
2 medium sized onions, sliced ·
3 tsp. ginger paste ·
1 tsp. garlic paste ·
2 tsp. red chilli powder ·
1 tsp. turmeric powder ·
salt to taste ·
250 ml yogurt ·
750 ml chicken stock ·
1/2 tsp. garam masala powder ·
a pinch of saffron ·

METHOD

Grind almonds, chironji and khuskhus to a fine paste.

Heat oil a pan and sauté sliced onions to golden brown colour.

Add ginger paste, garlic paste and sauté for two minutes.

Add red chilli powder and turmeric powder.

Add chicken pieces and stir-fry for five minutes.

Sprinkle a little water at intervals so that the masala does not burn.

Add salt.

Add the yogurt and cook further for a minute.

Add almond-chironji-khuskhus paste and cook for five minutes stirring continuously.

Pour in three cups of chicken stock and bring to a boil.

Once the mixture boils, cover and simmer for twenty minutes.

Once the chicken is cooked, add garam masala powder and saffron, stir and remove from heat.

Serve with garlic naan.

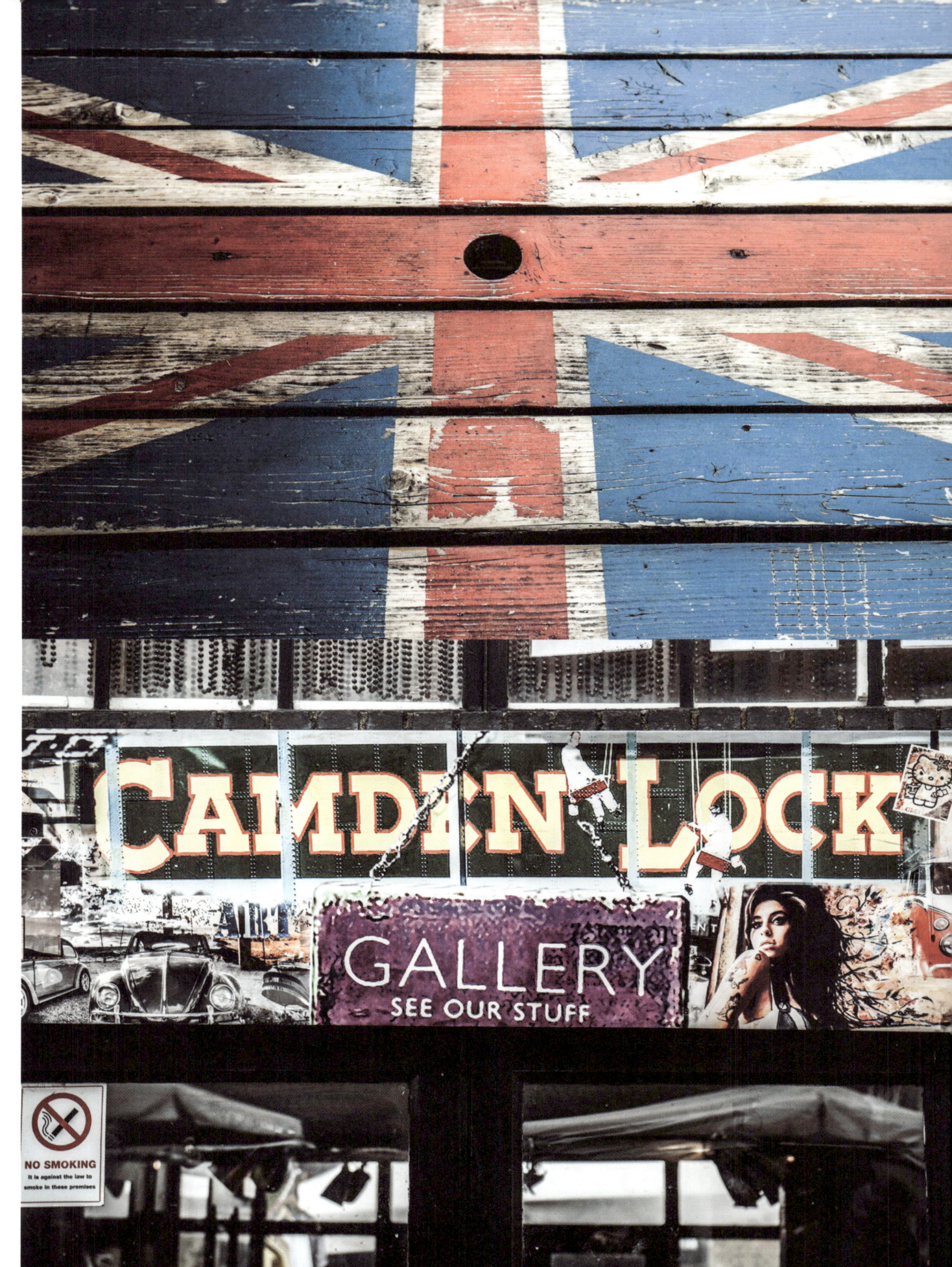

AND NOW FOR SOMETHING COMPLETELY DIFFERENT

You know that irresistible feeling you get when you see a coconut? When you just have to bang the two halves together rhythmically and pretend you're riding a horse, just like that scene in *Monty Python & the Holy Grail?* I certainly do; I just love the UK for all sorts of reasons and that film is one of them.

Although there isn't much I believe in, the story of King Arthur, his Excalibur and Camelot touches me in some way, and when I stood next to the Chalice Well in Glastonbury, I almost felt part of a childhood adventure story.

'A boiled peacock may seem to be alive'
When I was in Canterbury, looking at an illustrated version of the famous Canterbury Tales, a picture of a servant who was serving food to the future Queen Elizabeth I and her father King Henry VIII caught my eye. What I noticed about this mediaeval illustration was that he was serving a colourful, almost life-like peacock, feathers and all, on a large tray: magnificent, surreal and traditional at the same time. The illustration held me in its sway and I decided to do some research to discover the story behind it. In the course of my research, I came across the Magia naturalis (or Natural Magic in English of course), a scientific work by Giambattista della Porta, which was first published in Naples in 1558. It became so popular that it was reprinted five times in Latin, and was translated into Italian, French, Dutch and of course English too, in 1658. The books provide an insight into everyday questions people asked in those days; a sort of Harold McGee before he even existed.

In it, I found the following recipe, which

DINNER
BY heston blumenthal

Heston Blumenthal, who dared to be inspired by a phenomenal element of late-mediaeval gastronomy is principally famous for his worldwide awards and technically spectacular cuisine.

leaves little to the imagination: '*Kill a Peacock, either by thrusting a Quill into his brain from above, or else cut his throat, as you do for young Kids, that the blood may come forth. Then cut his skin gently from his throat unto his tail, and being cut, pull it off with his feathers from his whole body to his head. Cut off that with the skin, and legs, and keep it. Roast the Peacock on a spit. His body being stuffed with spices and sweet Herbs, sticking first on his breast Cloves, and wrapping his neck in a white Linen cloth. Wet it always with water, that it may never dry. When the Peacock is roasted, and taken from the spit, put him into his own skin again, and that he may seem to stand upon his feet, you shall thrust small Iron wires, made on purpose, through his legs, and set fast on a board, that they may not be discerned, and through his body to his head and tail. Some put Camphire in his mouth, and when he is set upon the table, they cast in fire. Platina shows that the same may be done with Pheasants, Geese, Capons, and other birds. And we observe these things among our guests.*'

A masterly idea, in which the trompe-l'oeil plays such an incredibly important role in a meal that it provides part of the entertainment too. The book is full of amazing recipes; it's my secret desire to cook these dishes one by one exactly as they are described and to decant the results into a book as a sort of illustrated *Magia Naturalis*. There are for instance phenomenal recipes such as 'and thus you have a Lordly dish' in which ten chickens are roasted next to each other on a spit and afterwards coated with a sort of pastry that is naturally coloured in ten different ways. I can already see the spectacular, colourful result in my mind's eye.

Heston Blumenthal

The contemporary chef who dared to be inspired by this phenomenal element of late-mediaeval gastronomy is principally famous for his worldwide awards and technically spectacular cuisine. But this brilliant Jewish man, with whom I share the same year of birth, is more profound than that.

When he woke up one morning in Provence, aged 16, he probably had no inkling that his life was about to take a dramatic turn. Or even that he had an appointment with culinary history that day. His parents took him to the Michelin-starred restaurant L'Oustau de Baumanière and it was there that he had the feeling of coming home. He not only felt inspired by the quality of the food, but by the entire sensory experience. The sound of nearby fountains, the crickets, the intense scent of flowering lavender, the atmosphere in the room while the waiters were carving the lamb: that was the world he wanted to become a part of. From that moment on, it was clear to him that he wanted to cook.

When he left school at 18, he dearly wanted to do something with the feeling he had had two years previously in the Provence and so, with no formal training, he became an apprentice to Raymond Blanc. He only stayed there a week, however, because he

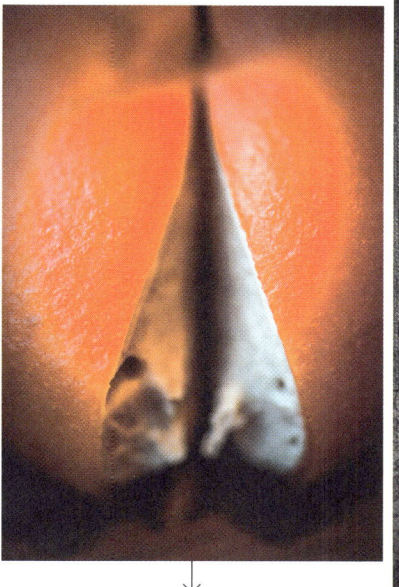

Meat fruit is a late mediaeval recipe. A sort of tromp-l'oeil: you see a mandarin in all its details, but the inside is a mousse made of chicken livres and foie gras.

wanted the freedom to do other things. He took on all sorts of jobs, but always left himself enough scope to teach himself the French classical repertoire. The pivotal moment came when he came across Harold McGee's *The Science and Lore of the Kitchen*. Blumenthal recognised a kindred spirit in McGee's stubborn philosophy, which challenges everything we take for granted, because that is his motto too: question everything.

Another important item in Blumenthal's oeuvre is that he is inspired by the gastronomic history of the British Isles, and this is where we see the link with the *Magia Naturalis*. He was given *The Vivendier*, a translation into modern-day English of this 15th-century cookery manuscript. His world was turned on its head by the light-heartedness and creativity of the recipes. Together with his scientific approach of questioning everything, this book formed the basis for his London venue, Dinner. His three mentors who – unknowingly – helped to lay the foundations for Dinner were Marc Meltonville, Richard Fitch and Ivan Day. After frequent consultations with these three food historians, Heston began devising recipes on the basis of historic, often mediaeval, dishes. A spectacular example is undoubtedly his Meat Fruit, which everyone thought involved a technical tour de force, but is actually a late mediaeval recipe that uses only a handful of ingredients. What you see is the form of a plum, an apple and a mandarin. The latter is a reference to the Mandarin oriental. The initial impression that it is all a gimmick disappears immediately after the first bite. It is a sort of tromp-l'oeil, similar to that found in art. You see a mandarin in all its details, but the inside is an unbelievably delicious mousse made of chicken livers and enriched with *foie gras*.

CHICKEN LIVER PARFAIT

A classic version of the masterpiece that has inspired probably thousands of chefs since the *Magia naturalis* first appeared.

INGREDIENTS

Makes 1 terrine
- 300 g chicken livers
- 300 g salted butter
- 3 large eggs
- 250 ml ruby port
- 250 ml brandy
- 2 cloves garlic
- 1 sprig thyme
- 2 small shallots
- salt and pepper

METHOD

In a pan, reduce the port and brandy together with the sliced garlic, thyme and shallots until it glazes, then sieve and set aside to cool down.

Clean the chicken livers of any membrane and place in a Thermomix together with the butter. Blitz until smooth at 37 °C.

Add eggs to liver mixture one by one, as well as the port reduction and season mix with salt and pepper. Sieve mixture to remove any impurities.

Line a terrine mould with cling film and pour mixture in. Then cook in a bain marie at 120 °C for 45-60 min. A good trick is to probe the centre of the parfait to check, we are looking for 62 °C.

Allow to chill overnight in the fridge, then slice and serve with toasted brioche and fruit chutney.

CHICKEN CAESAR SALAD

To sidestep Prohibition in the US, Cesare (Caesar) Cardini moved his restaurant from San Diego to Tijuana just after the end of the First World War. Cardini, born close to Lago Maggiore in 1896, had made the journey across the ocean with his brother Alex. It was very busy that evening, 4th July 1924, and the restaurant was full of enthusiastic partygoers. There were more guests than meals. But to honour the reputation Italians had and still have for hospitality, he decided to make a salad for his customers 'live' at a table, using all the ingredients he still had available – with the customary Italian flair of course. A week later, guests asked for the same salad again and within no time the salad had gone viral, as we would say today. The rest is history.

INGREDIENTS

- 500 g chicken skin
- olive oil
- salt and pepper
- half a loaf of yesterday's bread
- 4 small romaine lettuces
- 150 g 'Keens cheddar'

For the dressing
- 2 eggs
- 1 dash Chardonnay vinegar
- 1 tsp. English mustard
- 4 dashes Worcester sauce
- 2 dashes tabasco
- 1 large clove garlic
- 1 lemon
- 10 anchovy fillets
- 200 ml sunflower oil
- pinch cayenne pepper

METHOD

In a large frying pan, fry the chicken skins on a low heat in a little olive oil. This takes time, allow 20-25 minutes, but frying on a low heat will render the fat out of the chicken skin. When the skins are crispy and golden, remove and place on kitchen paper. Season with salt and pepper.

Blend the old bread into rough breadcrumbs and add to the pan containing the chicken fat. Fry them in the fat until golden brown, drain on paper and season.

Make the Caesar dressing; in a blender start with the eggs, mustard, vinegar, anchovies, garlic, lemon zest and juice and blend on full power; slowly add the sunflower oil until all has emulsified. Add the cayenne, Worcester sauce and tabasco and blitz again. Taste it and add more tabasco if you like it spicier.

Cut the romaine lettuce in half lengthways and place face down in a hot grill pan until golden brown. Remove from the pan and spread the dressing over, top with the chicken skin and fried bread and warm in the oven (180 °C) for 2 minutes. Grate the cheddar over the top and serve straight away.

ROAST CHICKEN AND SAGE STUFFING

INGREDIENTS

1 large free range chicken ·
1 clove garlic ·
1 onion, diced finely ·

For the filling
250 g pork mince ·
12 sage leaves ·
75 g brioche crumbs ·
75 g salted butter ·

METHOD

Sweat the onion in some olive oil until soft and sweet. Add the chopped garlic and cook for 2 more minutes.

Combine all the ingredients together until the stuffing comes together, then fill the cavity of the chicken with it.

Rub the stuffed chicken with olive oil, salt and pepper and place in a hot oven (200 °C) for 50-60 minutes. I prefer to roast a chicken for a shorter time but in a hotter oven to get a nice colour on the skin.

Rest the chicken for 15 minutes then serve with some roasted seasonal vegetables.

CHICKEN AND GRAPE STOVE POT

INGREDIENTS

4 corn-fed chicken breasts ·
olive oil ·
1 bunch tarragon ·
100 ml sour cream ·
1 bunch seedless white grapes ·

For the sauce
4 shallots ·
200 ml Riesling ·
200 ml chicken stock ·

METHOD

To make the sauce for this, slice the shallots and sweat until soft, then deglaze the pan with the Riesling. Reduce till the shallots glaze, then add the chicken stock. Reduce it by half, then add the sour cream.

Place the chicken breasts skin side down in a casserole with some olive oil and fry until deep golden in colour. Then turn them and deglaze the pan with more wine. You want the casserole to cool slightly before adding the sauce. Add the chopped bunch of tarragon and the grapes and allow the chicken to cook on the stove top, on a low heat for about 12 minutes.

↓ Michael perfectly personifies the modern British trend of sticking close to tradition, while being innovative and exciting nonetheless.

Michael Yates

You need a lot of guts to open a restaurant in Belgium specialising in British food. When I organised the first gastronomic weekends to London about 30 years ago, everyone thought I'd gone mad. You can't get any decent food in England... I think that nowadays everyone is aware that London especially is undisputedly one of the top five most interesting food destinations in the world. And yet British cuisine – in Belgium at any rate – still has a slightly negative connotation, which is pure nonsense of course. There is a whole generation of flamboyant top chefs who have set new international standards.

The former Michelin-starred restaurant Oud Sluis used to have a custom of getting a member of its staff to cook something special for the whole group after the Friday evening customers had gone, and it always turned into a party. Nick Bril, at that time still Sergio Herman's sous chef at Oud Sluis, asked me to do it once. Obviously very flattered, I accepted with pleasure. 'OK,' he said, 'the food needs to be ready after the kitchen has been cleaned on Friday, so serve the first course at 2 am.' It was a great evening and it was when I got to know a modest, mischievous guy who had just finished his first day at Oud Sluis. Yup, that was Michael Yates.

Born in Lancashire in the northwest of England, he began by washing dishes in a local Italian restaurant, but was soon bitten by the cookery bug. He was popular with Michelin-starred restaurants in the UK and he became sous chef at Martin Wishart in Edinburgh. He then decided that it was time to do something new and he took the decision to go to Oud Sluis where he stayed for three years as sous chef and found love with Marijke.

I was a fan of Michael's cooking right from the start. He perfectly personifies the modern British trend of sticking close to tradition, but nonetheless being innovative and exciting. He, like me, is a big fan of people like Marco Pierre White and Fergus Henderson, and you can taste that in his dishes. I for one am glad that I don't have to go as far as London to get the Lyle's or Clove Club experience: it is right here in Berchem, served up by Michael and Marijke.

Spatchcock

This is a popular way of cutting open a chicken with the aim of shortening the time it takes to cook and therefore avoiding the risk of the meat drying out. It is also sometimes called butterflying, but the correct term is spatchcock. The etymological origins of the word seem to suggest that it is an abbreviation of 'dispatch the cock', a term that summarises it nicely.

A spatchcock is also an old English name for a young cockerel, but the word is more commonly known as a cookery term. Spattlecock or spatchcock is a way of preparing a bird for stuffing or grilling by removing the backbone and the sternum and flattening the bird as fully as possible. Irish cookery books written in the 18th century were the first to mention this term.

TANDOORI POUSSIN

INGREDIENTS

- 4 poussins
- 2 red onions
- 4 red chillies
- 200g ginger
- 6 cloves garlic
- 1 tsp. cumin seeds
- 1 tsp. turmeric
- 1 tsp. tandoori masala powder
- 200 g yogurt
- 6 kaffir lime leaves
- zest and juice of 2 limes

METHOD

Spatchcock the poussins, in other words, remove the birds' backbones.

Combine all the other ingredients and blitz them in a food processor until you have a smooth paste/marinade.

Marinate the spatchcocked birds thoroughly with the marinade. This is best done at least 24 hours before cooking as it will flavour and tenderise the birds.

Cook the poussins on the barbecue, on a direct heat of 200 °C, until golden brown. This should take 5 to 10 minutes. Then move them to an indirect heat for a further 10 minutes until cooked through.

It is not entirely unexpected that Yates chooses an Indian dish here. After all, Chicken tikka masala, not fish & chips, has now become the most popular dish in the UK. It's a good illustration of the UK's fantastic multicultural legacy.

'Black Smoke - BBQ-Bar-Rooftop' in Antwerp produces wide-ranging redneck fare. Their weapons are two pitmasters, an American smoker, a fire pit, asadores and barbecues.

THE FIRST PITMASTERS WERE WOMEN

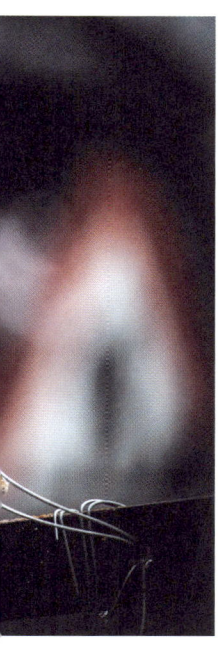

Of course many Americans think that the barbecue is an American invention. But that is sheer nonsense. Cooking meat over an open fire is as old as the human race itself.

If I imagine the invention of the barbecue, I see a tribe of primitive people warily following their noses through the smouldering ashes of a forest fire. Their keen olfactory organs have picked something up, the smell of roasting meat, but they don't know that yet. Depending on where this scene plays out, the air might also fill with the smell of herbs. All of a sudden, they see the source of this lovely smell: the burning carcass of a wild boar. They cautiously touch the animal's side, then lick their fingers and discover the sensational taste of fat and meat produced by the Maillard reaction. This magical blend of hot proteins, melted fat and creamy collagen is probably the very first thing these primitive people became addicted to, straight after the first bite.

Cooked meat made it easier for all mammals to take energy from food, and with the availability of more calories, the evolution of larger brains began. Cooked meat can also be eaten much more quickly than raw meat and so more time was freed up for hunting and for developing social skills. Humans developed flatter feet and narrower hips to run faster and they domesticated dogs to help them hunt. Once the first primitive farms were established, the animals that people found to be tastiest were kept close by. The social and family structure began to take shape: men were hunters and women cooked, so the first pitmasters were women.

THE FLYING CHICKEN

INGREDIENTS

- 1 chicken
- 30 g coarse sea salt
- 30 g black pepper, cracked
- 2 lemons, cut into quarters
- bulb of garlic
- a few sprigs of rosemary
- fresh thyme
- oregano

METHOD

Rub the coarse sea salt and the black pepper into the chicken cavity.

Stuff it with fresh herbs and the lemon. Tie up the chicken well with wire and leave a space to stick in the meat hook that is hanging on ropes. Light a fire, hang the chicken about a metre above it.

Leave it to cook slowly above the fire so that it can absorb the smoke thoroughly until the core temperature of the breast is 70 °C and that of the thighs 75 °C.

Barbecue in the Bible
The Hebrew Old Testament contains the very first detailed plan for building a barbecue. Exodus 27, which we think was written between 1300 and 1500 BC, tells of Moses, after he had received the Ten Commandments, instructing his followers to build an altar in which animals would be burnt as offerings. It is extremely detailed, describing meat hooks, firepans, pots for ashes and all manner of sophisticated material for tying the animal neatly to the 'barbecue'. The altar had no wheels, but there were poles on each side so that it could be carried with ease.

Exodus 29 gives instructions for sacrificing a young bull and roasting it over the fire, clearly describing the delicious flavour of this offering to God, who apparently was satisfied with the aroma alone. Moses' brother Aaron and the priest were however permitted to eat as much as they liked...

Leviticus 1 sounds more like a cookery book with its instructions for sacrificing bulls, doves, sheep, goats, fruit, maize and bread. It states clearly that God would not settle for the less noble parts of the meat. This is probably the origin of the kosher dietary laws...

Low and slow smoke roasting
The English essayist and humourist Charles Lamb wrote an interesting and above all humorous perspective on the origins of low and slow smoke roasting in 1822. He related the tale of the Chinese farmer, Bo-Bo, who accidentally burned down his father's pig shed many years ago. Bo-Bo thus discovered the method of smoking and roasting meat slowly and began a career as an arsonist, burning down every pig shed in his area whenever he had the urge to eat smoked roast pork.

For centuries, of course, Indians have been frying meat in ceramic urns heated by coal, called *tandoor,* and descriptions of a *kamado* in Japan, a similar ceramic urn for cooking meat, date back as many as 3000 years.

Texas
You can find no one prouder of his barbecue skills than a Texan. Texas has a real barbecue tradition and anyone who takes barbecuing seriously must spend some time travelling around here, stopping at the many barbecue institutes.

The tradition of smoking meat was introduced into Texas by the German and Czech immigrants who arrived here in the middle of the 19th century. It started as a way of preserving excess meat more easily, but it soon became a tradition in Texas, attracting all-comers.

Barbecue styles in Texas can be split along the lines of four regions: East, Central, South and western Texas. The most well-known and distinct are those of Central and East Texas. Griffin Smith, an authority on the barbecue, puts a dividing line

between the two styles running from Columbus and Hearne northwards between Dallas and Fort Worth.

The end of the American Civil War and the abolition of slavery in 1865 marked the birth of the East Texas barbecue style, which is really a cross-over product from the African-American community. The East Texas style involves cooking meat over hickory wood after marinating it in a sweet tomato-based sauce. When the meat falls off the bone it is considered cooked. In Central Texas a dry rub is applied to the meat before it is cooked on an indirect source of heat, usually pecan wood or oak. Inhabitants of western Texas prefer mesquite wood and in the south they make liberal use of thick molasses-type sauces which keep the meat very moist.

Pitmasters (BBQ)

Anyone who takes a barbecue seriously needs a pitmaster. A pitmaster's job is not easy: it requires dedication and getting up early, long evenings by the pit, and so on. If he wants fantastic results, he needs to stay close to the pit.

Barbecuing in Belgium is generally done at family parties or in a lidded Big Green Egg in one or other design restaurant, but now there is finally a restaurant where this ancient cooking technique has been elevated to an art. Other countries already have their barbecue legends of course, such as Fette Sau in Brooklyn, The Beast in Paris and Etxebarri in Spanish Basque country. They guarantee a gourmet barbecue experience.

The innovative catering entrepreneur, Kaspar Stuart, himself a fervent frequenter of barbecue restaurants all over the world, has finally given Antwerp its 'Black Smoke, BBQ Bar Rooftop' with two pitmasters. Mattias Jacobs & Vadim Vesters do nothing by halves. They have introduced an all-encompassing redneck kitchen with a modern twist, strong flavours and delicious barbecue influences: convivial family-style meals which are ideal for sharing. Big is beautiful.

Their weapons are an American smoker, fire pit, *asadores* and barbecues.
They are introducing Belgium to quality and diversity never seen before in this much underestimated art of cooking. Gastronomic barbecuing is very satisfying, and they feel right at home with it. Their cooking is unique and clever and presents flavours that will surprise the Belgian pallet. Their subtle chicken creations prove that a barbecue can be more than large slabs of dead cow.

SOUTHERN PRIDE SMOKED WINGS

INGREDIENTS

5 wings per person

Dry rub (300g)
- 60 g lemon pepper mix
- 40 g paprika powder
- 20 g smoked paprika powder
- 20 g salt
- 50 g granulated sugar
- 20 g caster sugar
- 30 g garlic powder
- 20 g onion powder
- 1 Tbsp. finely ground black pepper
- 1 tsp. chili powder
- 2 Tbsp. dried basil
- 1 Tbsp. dried thyme
- 1 Tbsp. dried rosemary
- some bourbon

Blue cheese dip
- 100 g blue cheese
- 1 clove of garlic
- 3 Tbsp. mayonnaise
- 1 Tbsp. lemon juice
- 2 Tbsp. finely chopped shallot
- 4 Tbsp. sour cream
- 5 drops of tabasco chipotle sauce

METHOD

Mix all these ingredients together carefully until you have a cohesive mass.

Apply the dry rub to the wings.

Place them in the smoker at 105 °C, using cherry wood to create the smoke. Cherry wood produces a slightly sweeter smoky flavour and turns the meat darker than other woods. It is ideal for cooking chicken and other ingredients that only need to cook for a short time.

Smoke the wings for about 45 minutes to an hour until their core temperature is 75 °C.

Spray the wings three times with bourbon as they smoke.

Serve with sticks of celery and the blue cheese dip.

PULLED CHICKEN SANDWICH

INGREDIENTS

1 chicken ·
50 g dry rub, as described above ·
2 lemons, cut into quarters ·
bulb of garlic ·
a few sprigs of rosemary ·
fresh thyme ·
oregano ·
a few bay leaves ·
marinated red onion ·

Crispy chicken skin
500 g chicken skins ·
1 litre chicken stock ·
300 g tapioca flour ·
salt and pepper ·
mixture of spices for chicken ·
(paprika, salt, onion powder, thyme,
garlic powder, coriander, black pepper,
chili powder, basil)

To finish
slices of bread or bread rolls ·
marinated red onion ·
barbecue sauce ·

METHOD

Boil the chicken skins in the stock until they are completely cooked. Heat them in a Thermomix with the tapioca flour and mix for 30 minutes at 100 °C. Season the mixture to taste with salt, pepper and mixed herbs.

After mixing, spread it out thinly on greaseproof paper.

Bake this dough for 45 minutes in a dry oven at 160 °C.

Rub mixed herbs all over the whole chicken; stuff the chicken with the quarters of lemon, garlic, fresh thyme, rosemary and bay leaves.

Place the chicken on the smoker heated to 105 °C for about 1.5 to 2 hours until the white meat (breast) reaches a core temperature of 70°C.

Pull the chicken apart completely and mix it all into the barbecue sauce.

Build up the sandwich with marinated red onion, a crispy chicken skin and pulled chicken in whichever quantities you like.

BEERCAN CHICKEN

INGREDIENTS

1 chicken ·
2 cans of beer ·
50 g dry rub, as described above ·
dried rosemary to taste ·

METHOD

Inject beer into the chicken's breast and thighs.

Heat the beer can on the barbecue so that the beer can evaporate once the chicken is sitting on top of it.

Season the chicken completely with the dry rub.

When the beer starts to boil in the can, place the chicken on top of it, pulling out its two legs to form a tripod with the beer can on the grill.

When the chicken is over the heat, throw some rosemary onto the coals at regular intervals to give the chicken a scented, smoky flavour.

Cook the chicken for about an hour until the core temperature of the breast is 70 °C and that of the thighs 75 °C.

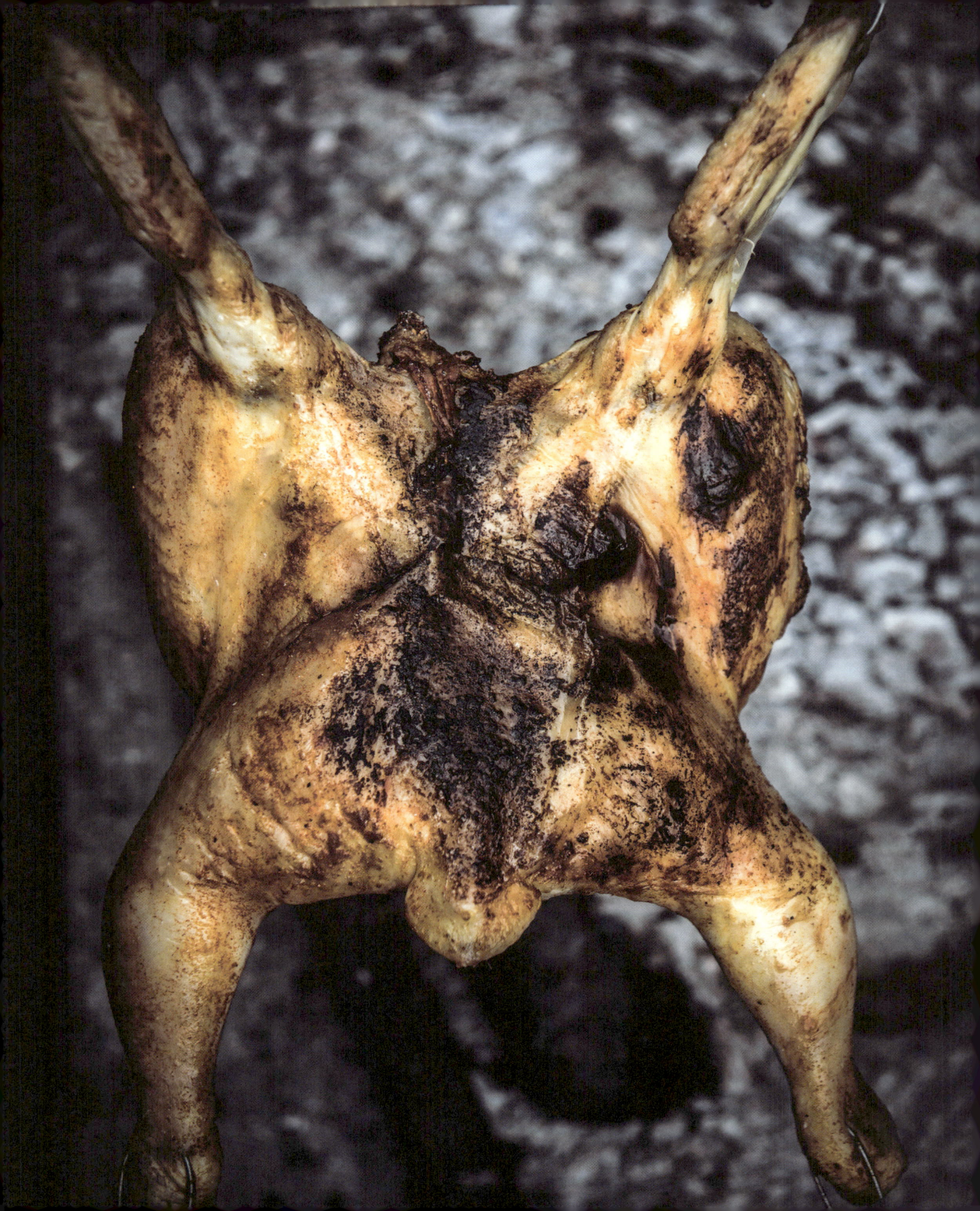

CHICKEN ON ASADO CROSS

INGREDIENTS

1 chicken
30 g coarse sea salt
30 g black pepper, cracked

Seasoned oil
olive oil
lemon thyme
rosemary
bay leaves
basil
oregano
garlic

METHOD

Seasoned oil

Mix all the ingredients together and leave to stand for at least 24 hours.

Chicken

Cut the chicken in half along the breastbone and open it out so that it can be fastened to the cross.

Rub the chicken with coarse sea salt and pepper and brush with the seasoned oil.

Light a fire using cherry wood to produce a sweet smoky flavour and the right colour.

Place the cross with the open chicken hanging on it around the fire such that the heat and smoke from the fire will reach it. Don't make the fire too big, but make sure it smokes well.

Leave the chicken to cook slowly from a distance until the core temperature of the breast is 70 °C and that of the thighs 75 °C.

BARBECUE VS BARBACOA

People in the southernmost tip of South Texas, the Rio Grande Valley, often talk of *barbacao*. Although this is obviously the Spanish word for barbecue, it refers to cooking meat in a dug-out pit filled with hot coals. Usually a whole animal wrapped in maguey leaves is placed across it, and the meat is left to smoulder slowly.

Asadores

Asado is a Spanish term that refers to both a series of barbecue techniques and to attending a barbecue. It is also a term used for barbecue in Spanish-speaking South America. The genuine, traditional asado takes place over a pit in which a fire is lit using local wood. The *asadores*, a sort of cross construction on which the meat is crucified, so to speak, is placed above the fire so that the heat can penetrate all parts of the meat and it can cook evenly.

UNESCO-protectoraat

South American cookery is rarely taken seriously in our country. What is usually served under the banner of South American and especially Mexican food is an absolute travesty. Mexican cuisine is probably the most misunderstood in the world. Nonetheless, it was the first to be awarded the fervently coveted UNESCO world heritage protectorate.

Mexican cuisine is first and foremost a successful marriage between the native

Meso-American style of cookery and the mainly Spanish influences as a consequence of the Spanish conquest of the Aztec Empire. As befits true imperialists, the Spaniards tried – relatively unsuccessfully – to impose their own cuisine and eventually the ingredients and the cookery techniques spontaneously began to mix, producing a greater whole than the sum of its parts. The emergence of many local variants such as Oaxaca, Veracruz and Yucatan came about in the same way.

Mole poblano

Mole poblano is one of the world's greatest recipes, in which the meat from chicken thighs is stewed in a complex mixture of chicken stock, various varieties of chili peppers, aromatic spices, old bread, nuts and cocoa. It was first created when nuns at the Santa Rosa convent in Puebla de Los Angeles were in a panic because the archbishop was coming to visit the convent and they had nothing to give him. The chicken in the deep, dark sauce turned out to be amazingly delicious.

The secret is a real *mole madre,* a sort of mother-ship that is kept continually on the heat and to which the right ingredients are added at just the right time. The flavour of the sauce becomes more and more intense; *mole madres* that have been on the go for a thousand days or more are genuinely no exception.

Nikkei cuisine

Is it a *Nikkei Burajirujin* or is it a *Nipo-Brasileiro?* The largest Japanese community outside Japan lives in Liberdade, a district in São Paulo. The first Japanese arrived in this Brazilian city in 1908.

After the abolition of mainly black slavery in 1850, Brazil tried to entice other workers to the country to work in the cradles of its most important export product: coffee plantations. They were keen to encourage Europeans to make the country 'whiter'. But the poor working conditions led to many countries calling a halt to emigration to Brazil.

The end of the feudal system in Japan resulted in widespread poverty and unemployment at the end of the 19th century. Many Japanese decided to try their luck in Brazil. This culminated in the signing of a treaty between Japan and Brazil to make it easier to migrate between the two countries. The first 790 people arrived at Kasato Maru from Kobe in 1908. Almost all of them were coffee plantation owners. By 1940, there were 164,000, most of whom invariably ended up in São Paulo.

Between 1920 and 1950, Japanese food was only served in São Paulo in huge refectories specifically for Japanese people. The first real restaurant, in Liberdade, was called Okinasushi and it opened in 1950; up until then, the locals of São Paulo had remained relatively immune to Japanese influences. The restaurant changed all that and signalled the start of a brisk, harmonious and amicable easing of the gastronomical cultural differences.

HOLY SHIT!
TAPATÍO
TIGER
SAUCE
THE ORIGINAL
ILEGAL MEZCAL
TEQUILA Y COCINA
CARACAS
CARACAS

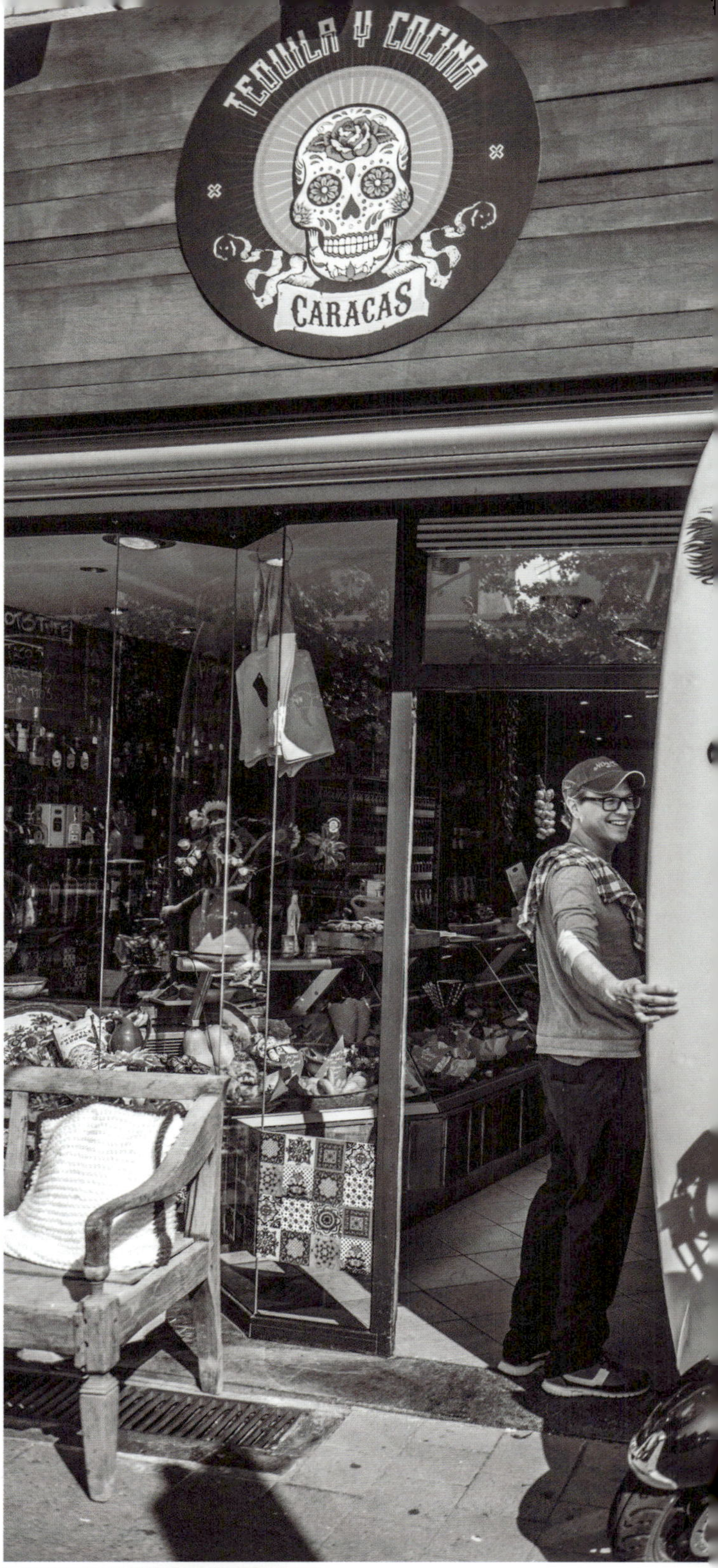

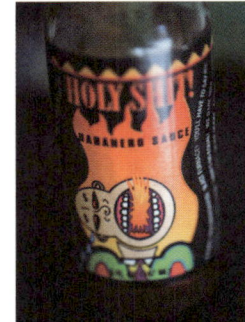

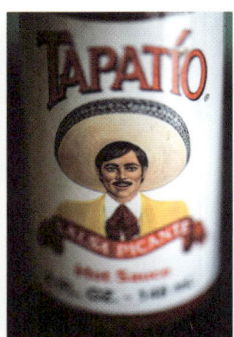

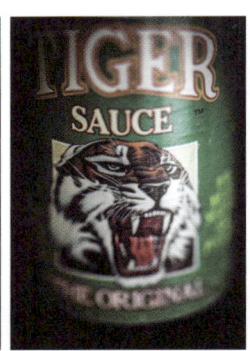

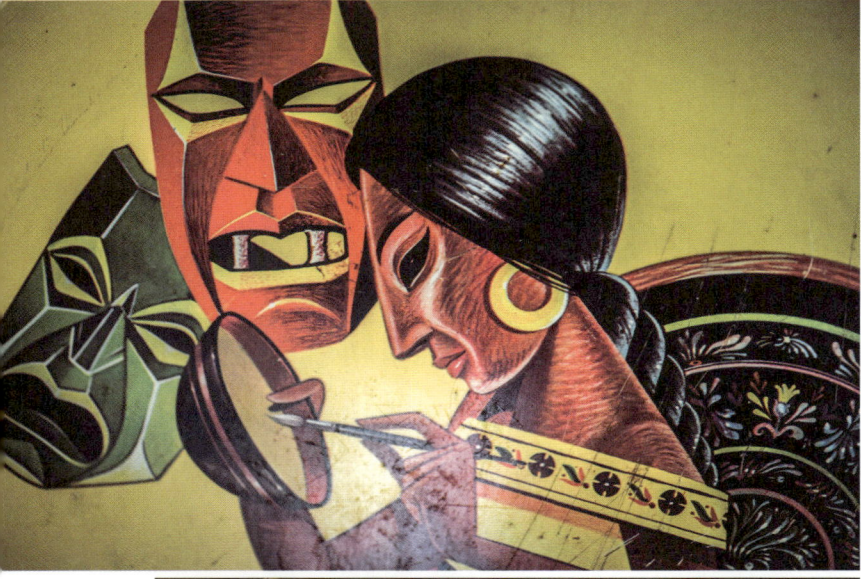

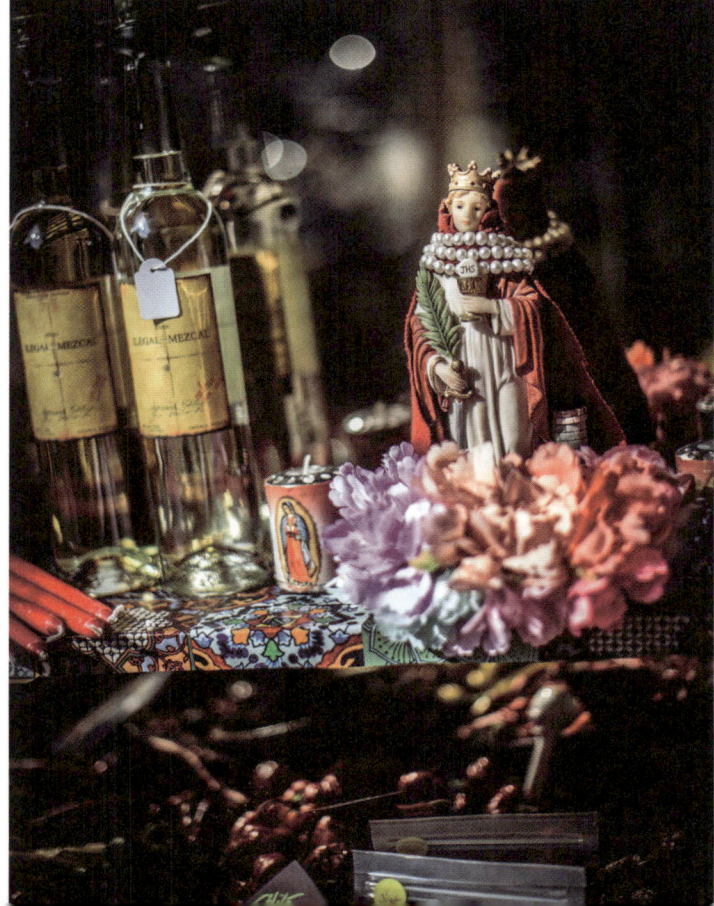

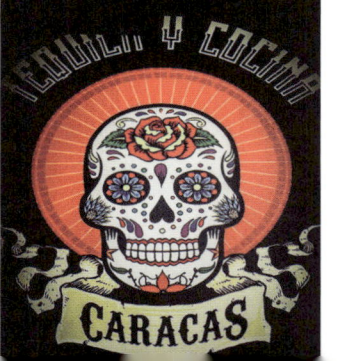

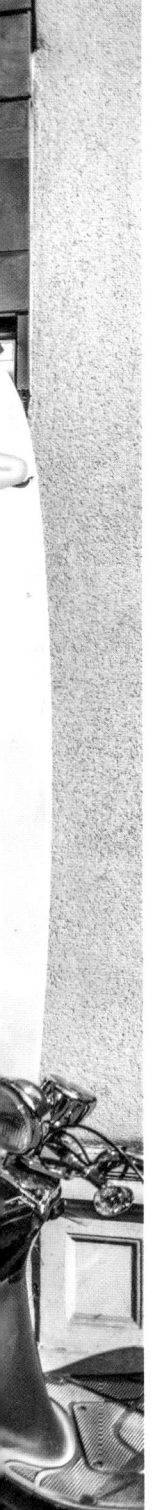

It was not until 1981 that Kiyomi Watanabe, whose parents earned their living fishing, opened the first Japanese restaurant outside Liberdade, in Bladder to be exact, where many other cultures already had restaurants, including lots of Italians. The Japanese/Brazilian gastronomic fusion thus only took place quite recently and took a lot more doing than in Peru for example.

Peruvian cuisine was put on the menu on a global scale by Nobu. Nobuyuki Matsuhisa or Nobu as everyone calls him, is truly phenomenal. When he was seven, his father was killed in a tragic car accident. His mother was left to bring up Nobu and his two brothers all on her own. He went to work at Matsue Sushi in Shinjuku at quite a young age, where a rich Peruvian businessman recognised his talent. In 1973, when he was 24, Nobu and the businessman opened a Japanese restaurant in Lima. Because he was unable to find the ingredients in Peru that were easily available in Japan, he developed his own style of cooking by inventing a sort of fusion in which Peruvian ingredients are perfectly incorporated into Japanese dishes. It turned out to be a unique style too, because it is only now, thirty years later, that the crème de la crème of Michelin-starred chefs are beginning to realise the benefits of Peruvian influences.

Bart Huybrechts

Before Bart and his wife Stefanie went to Los Angeles on their honeymoon, they came to ask my advice. Little did I know that I would be responsible for part of their future. I sent them downtown, where there is a magnificent Mexican market between The Flight of the Angels and the iconic Bradbury building: Grand Central Market. Go to the stall with the roast goats' heads and ask for a *taco a pastor*, I had written. Bart and his wife were completely captivated by the Mexican feel of downtown LA and were enchanted by the complex flavours of this style of cooking. So enchanted were they that they studied the material in depth and opened the first serious outpost of Mexican cuisine – and by extension South America – in Antwerp.

Bart, a chef of many talents, who has spent a large part of his professional career setting things up for great chefs and living in their shadow, was now able to take centre stage with a refined and refreshing vision of these unsung cuisines. He has formed an alliance with the Latino community in Antwerp whose members are only too happy to share their parents' and grandparents' expertise and recipes with this enthusiastic Belgian who is honouring their community.

BASIC MOLE POBLANO

INGREDIENTS

Makes 1.5 litre sauce for about 1 kg meat depending on the method.

Sauce
- coconut oil
- 2 shallots, shredded
- 2 onions, shredded
- 2 cloves of garlic, shredded
- small tin of tomato puree
- 1/2 block of *achiote (annatto extract)* or a small pinch of saffron
- 50 g oven-roasted peanuts, ground to a powder
- 20 g oven-roasted pickled almonds, ground
- 4 peeled tomatoes, chopped roughly
- 2 peeled red *ancho poblano* chili peppers, with stalk and seeds removed (alternative: red pointed pepper)
- 1/2 Trinidad scorpion chocolate chili pepper, with stalk and seeds removed (alternative: a small very spicy chili pepper)
- 1 litre chicken stock (preferably a strong, dark, gelatinous chicken stock)
- 2 old, dried out corn tortillas
- 1 Tbsp. dark chocolate 80% cocoa, chopped finely

METHOD

Use a large, wide pan with a thick base.

Heat some coconut oil in the pan and sauté the onions, shallots and garlic. Add the tomato puree and fry until it changes colour slightly. Add the block of achiote.

Add the roasted spices. Add the ground nuts and fry them briefly on a high heat.

Add the peeled tomatoes, poblano chili peppers and Trinidad chili pepper.

Pour in the chicken stock. Cover with the dried up tortillas and put a lid on the pan. Leave to simmer on the lowest heat for 45 minutes.

Stir the corn tortillas into the sauce and boil the sauce down if necessary. Skip this step if your sauce is thick enough. Remove the pan from the heat. Add the chocolate and mix until melted. Beat the sauce using a hand-held mixer.

POLLO CON MOLE

INGREDIENTS

- 1 kg chicken thigh meat with skin
- a few Tbsp. roasted sesame seeds

For the dried spice mixture *(mole)*
- 1 tsp. coriander seeds
- 1/2 stick of cinnamon
- 1 star anise
- 2 cloves
- 2 dried *ancho* chilies, seeds and stalks removed
- 2 dried *pasilla* chilies, seeds and stalks removed

METHOD

Mole

Roast all the spices in a dry frying pan with no fat until they release their aroma. Grind them once they have cooled (preferably in a small blender or electric coffee grinder) and then pass through a fine sieve. Only use the dried powder.

Chicken

Rub some of the dried spice mixture and salt into the meat and fry the pieces of chicken until they are golden. Moisten with some chicken stock and add as much mole as you wish. Garnish with some roasted sesame seeds.

STICKY CHILI CHICKEN WINGS

INGREDIENTS

12 chicken wings ·
4 Tbsp. coconut oil ·
Yucateco black label hot sauce ·
(Alternative: tabasco chipotle)

For the mole poblano glaze
0.5 litre water ·
5 dried and smoked chipotles (chili peppers) ·
200 g cane sugar ·
juice of 1 lime ·

METHOD

Chicken wings

Fry six chicken wings (in three pieces) in the coconut oil until cooked and crisp.

Remove the excess coconut oil and wing tips; moisten with drops of Yucateco black label hot sauce.

Add a few tablespoons of mole poblano glaze, as much as is needed to coat the wings completely.

Mole poblano glaze

Boil the smoked chipotles in the water for 15 minutes. Remove the chipotles. Cool, remove seeds and stalks. Add sugar; reduce until you are left with runny syrup.

Moisten with lime juice. Add the chipotles and mole. Mix with a handheld mixer.

EMPANADAS WITH CHICKEN LIVER AND MOLE POBLANO

Empanadas can be found in various forms all over South America. White or yellow maize flour is generally used in Central America, while the further south you go, you find more puff pastry or bread dough. To make it more convenient for home cooks, we recommend using puff pastry. The version with maize flour requires a tortilla press.

INGREDIENTS

Makes 12 empanadas with 50 g filling
- 2 shallots, shredded
- 1 clove of garlic, shredded
- 4 Tbsp. coconut oil
- 200 g minced chicken
- 100 g chicken livers, in pieces
- 5 Tbsp. chicken stock
- 2 Tbsp. red kidney beans boiled in stock
- 2 Tbsp. sultanas
- 4 Tbsp. mole poblano
- a few sheets of puff pastry
- 2 egg yolks

METHOD

Sauté the shallots and garlic in coconut oil.

Brown the minced chicken in a little coconut oil on a high heat and fry the chicken livers quickly too. Moisten with the chicken stock.

Add the beans and sultanas. Now add four tablespoons of *mole poblano* and cook for five minutes. Puree coarsely.

Cut out 10 circles 15 centimetres in diameter from a sheet of frozen puff pastry. Prick a few holes in the pastry with a fork. Brush the edges with beaten egg yolk, arrange 50 grams of lukewarm filling just below the centre of the circle and fold over. Press the edges together with a fork, brush with egg yolk and place on a non-stick baking sheet or on greaseproof paper. Bake for 12 minutes in a fan oven at 180 °C.

CHICHARRON DE POLLO

INGREDIENTS

chicken skins ·
fine salt ·
dried spice mixture *(see p. 136)* ·
water ·
a few sheets of kitchen paper ·
deep fat fryer with beef fat ·

METHOD

Put the chicken skins on to boil in plenty of cold, salted water. Boil for a few minutes then remove the skins, rinse them well under cold water and remove anything that isn't skin (any pieces of meat, feathers or bone).

Open out the skins and lay them on kitchen paper, sprinkle a little fine salt on the upper side and then pat it completely dry a few minutes later. Do this very thoroughly so that no water remains in any cavities.

Press the skins into the basket of the deep fat fryer to prevent them from curling up too much when frying. Fry them for five to ten minutes in clean fat at 150 °C.

Drain them on kitchen paper, patting them gently on all sides; sprinkle with salt and the dried spice mixture. They will keep for a few days at room temperature in an airtight box lined with some kitchen paper.

SOPA DE PATAS

INGREDIENTS

- 1 kg chicken legs
- *(use black leg chicken (poulet noir) if possible)*
- 2 large Spanish onions
- 2 winter carrots
- coconut oil
- 1 Tbsp. achiote
- 2 Spanish serrano peppers
- 2 cloves of garlic
- 1 Tbsp. dried spice mixture (see above)
- 1 litre strong chicken stock
- 2 corn on the cob
- 250 g dried pinto beans, soaked overnight and then boiled until just tender in salted water
- 4 plump, ripe tomatoes
- 1 sweet potato
- salt and pepper to taste
- 1 bunch of fresh coriander
- 1 Tbsp. dried tepin peppers

METHOD

Wash the chicken legs well in cold water.

Put them on to boil in plenty of lightly salted cold water. Bring to the boil; skim off the scum, and drain.

Wash the chicken legs again thoroughly and, using a sharp knife, remove the nails and callouses under the ball of the foot. Do this very scrupulously because a lot of dirt can gather in the callouses. Pull the tendons out of the leg by grasping them with kitchen tongs and giving them a sharp pull. If you do it properly, you will have two tendons about 10 centimetres long and two about 5 centimetres long. The legs are now ready to use.

Cut the onion and washed carrot into large chunks; sauté them in plenty of coconut oil.

After a few minutes, add the achiote, chili peppers, finely chopped garlic and dried spice mixture. Cover with a lid and braise on a low heat.

Now add the chicken legs and the chicken stock. Simmer for half an hour on a low heat, removing as much scum as possible as it forms. Scum always contains dirt and impurities. As you do so, try not to remove too much of the oil that floats to the top. It contains the gelatine and collagen from the legs to which healing properties are ascribed.

Now add the large corn on the cob, sweet potato, pinto beans and peeled tomatoes. Bring to the boil and simmer for 20 minutes. Continue to remove any scum where necessary.

Season to taste and, if necessary, add some strong chicken stock to water it down a bit. Just before serving, stir in some roughly chopped coriander leaves. Finely dice the coriander stalks (brunoise), crumble some tepin peppers between your fingers and sprinkle both over the soup as a garnish.

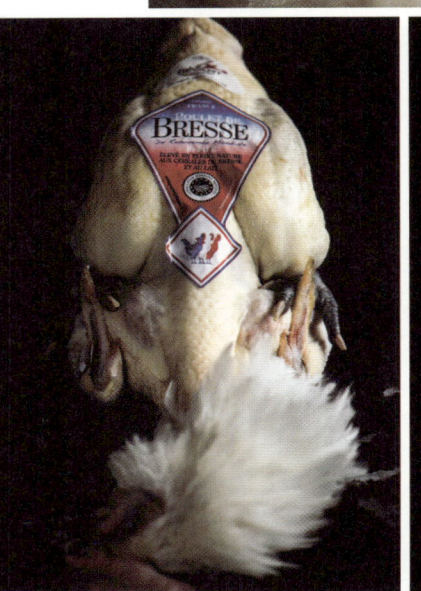

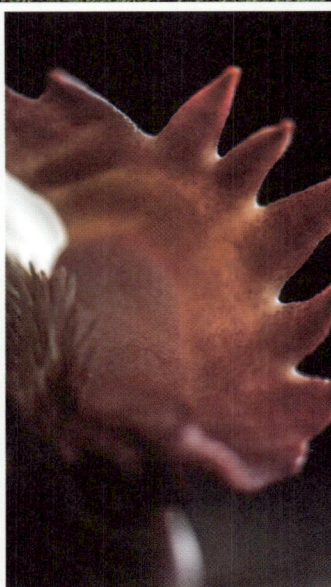

16 m2 of free space, there are wild herbs in the meadows, acupuncture to combat stress prior to slaughter, old kamut grain, you name it; these chickens lead a life fit for a king before they end up in the pot.

Chicken with a pedigree
The story of the exceptional, regal fowl now known as *poulet de Bresse* began in 1591, when this white bird was first mentioned in the city records of Bourg-en-Bresse. When Henry IV stopped there after an accident with his coach, he tasted the meat and was immediately enchanted by it and demanded that meat from Bresse chickens be included in court menus.

The Marquis de Treffort received a gift of two boxes of these superb chickens in thanks for halting a plundering army from the Savoy but they achieved everlasting glory when Jean-Anthelme Brillat-Savarin (1755-1826) described the chickens as the queen of chickens and the chicken of kings.

The next highpoint for this chicken was reached on 22 December 1936. A controlled designation of origin was introduced, an actual *Appellation d'origine contrôlée*. The specifications are very strictly regulated and this aristocrat among modern birds for the table is quite simply the best chicken there is. Needless to say, there are good, very good and excellent producers. And the greatest, the supreme producer, is a... Belgian!

Never call a *poulet de Bresse* just a chicken
I'm no good when it comes to chronology, but about 25 years ago I had an excited phone call from a good friend telling me he had bought a farmhouse and some land in Bresse and asking me if I'd like to go with him when he went to pick up the keys. It so happens that Bresse lies between two of my favourite wine regions, Jura and Bourgogne, and one of my favourite restaurants is in Arbois: Jean-Paul Jeunet. So I didn't take long to decide.

My friend's purchase turned out to be a magnificent ruin of a traditional Bresse farmhouse with a sizeable plot of land next to it. And that's where the story began: old varieties of grain, pigs in a large, enclosed section of an old oak wood, an incredible vegetable garden and, of course, *poulet de Bresse*. No one breeds chickens with the same dedication and vision in Bresse as these people. They have virtually created their own *cahier de charges*, much stricter and better than that of the *appellation*. It is a culinary jigsaw in which everything falls neatly into place. It might be mad, but each chicken here has 16 m2 of free space, there are wild herbs in the meadows, acupuncture to combat stress prior to slaughter, old kamut grain, you name it; these chickens lead a life fit for a king before they end up in the pot.

Through my contacts in the Belgian restaurant world I was able to help them find the right people who would understand this farm-to-table philosophy and would treat them well. What they were doing in those days was truly innovative, not yet a

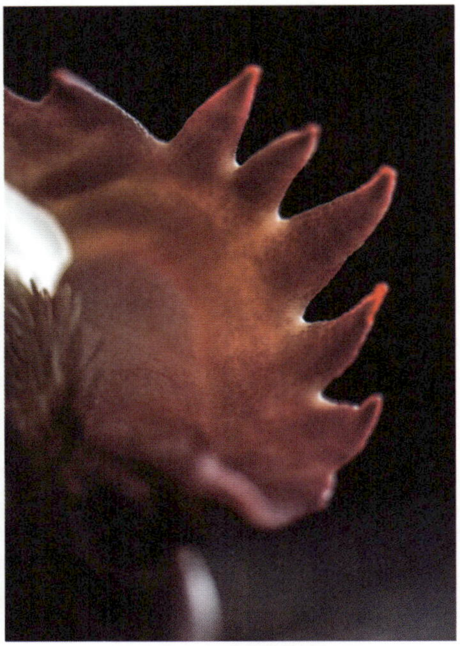

well-trodden trend. Brasserie Latem and Dock's Café at once wanted to be part of the story. And when the quasi-perfect 72-ha biotope was functioning almost like a labour-intensive *perpetuum mobile,* and the owners made it known that they wanted to start taking things more easily, Dimitri de Cuyper, their best customer and partner in Ferme Le Devant, took the initiative to acquire it. Dimitri continues to invest in quality and sustainability and that has proven to be a very good decision. He is at the top of the pecking order.

You can now eat the best chicken in the world, in all sorts of shapes, flavours and colour in La Quincaillerie (Brussel), 't Pakhuis (Gent) and Brasserie Dock's (Antwerp).

Patrick Verheire

What a pleasure to see a true craftsman and consequently a professional at work. Working with products like those from Le Devant is a challenge, but also a genuine pleasure for a born chef like Patrick Verheire. He revealed to me that he already has 38 years under his belt and you can see that in the precision of his methods and mastery of his cooking. He radiates experience and you can taste it too in the essential elements, such as his *fonds* and sauces.

His kitchen produces signature dishes and dynamic dishes. A signature dish is one that is always on the menu, irrespective of the season, such as his prawn croquette or a good piece of red meat. In addition to these, there are the dynamic items that change with the seasons. But what fascinates me most is the supply of carcasses and vegetables from Le Devant. That introduces quite distinct dynamics into the kitchen, because a whole animal has to be dealt with. You have to pickle and make pâté: a real nose-to-tail process. One of Patrick's virtues is his adamant persistence in letting guests choose *à la carte*. That makes the work very demanding, given the number of covers at Brasserie Dock's, but it is the crowning glory of his work. No conveyor belt work here and no dull, 90% *mise-en-place* menus.

This unequalled professional deserves more recognition. People don't seem to understand that a brasserie kitchen of this calibre – and there are only a few in Belgium – requires the same effort and volume of work as a classic Michelin-starred place. I take my hat off to this modest man with a big heart and enormous talent.

Pozharsky

Tradition has it that Pozharsky was one of Tsar Nicolas I's favourite innkeepers. He used to serve a sort of veal or chicken cutlet by mixing minced meat with butter and bone marrow to form the shape of a cutlet and then, after dipping it in breadcrumbs, frying it in butter.

The inn in Torzhok, somewhere between Moscow and St Petersburg, was a popular place for coaches to stop where horses were professionally cared for. In one of Alexander Pushkin's letters written in 1826, he mentions that he liked to stop in Torzhok to eat Pozharsky's fantastic fried cutlets. The Tsar even invited the innkeeper's wife, Darya Pozharsky to come and serve this piece of meat at court. Georges Auguste Escoffier himself immortalised this dish by including it in *Le guide culinaire*. The original recipe used veal, but the version with chicken became increasingly popular and for a long time featured on Alain Ducasse's menu in Monaco.

CLASSIC DISHES

CASSEROLE OF SAUTÉED CHICKEN WITH ARTICHOKE, SAGE AND PRESERVED LEMON

INGREDIENTS

For the mirepoix
- onion
- carrot
- celery
- thyme
- bay leaf
- 3 cloves of garlic

- 1 ready-to-cook *poulet de Bresse* (approx. 1.80 kg)
- a few sage leaves
- 1 preserved lemon
- 100 ml dry white wine
- 100 ml brown chicken fond
- 4 poivrade artichokes
- 4 turnips
- 8 baby carrots
- 12 fresh cocktail onions
- 100 g butter beans
- a few knobs of butter

METHOD

Start by stewing the mirepoix. Season the chicken and brown in a frying pan.

Transfer the chicken to a saucepan and add the sage and the preserved lemon. Moisten with the wine and the brown chicken fond.

Bring to the boil and then leave to simmer gently.

Peel the dark outer leaves off the artichoke, cut lengthwise into quarters and remove the chokes. Cook them 'à la barigoule': with vegetables, white wine and chicken fond.

Peel the turnips and cut into quarters. Blanch them, the baby carrots and the cocktail onions until just tender. Cook the butterbeans.

Remove the chicken from the sauce when it is cooked. Finish off the sauce with knobs of butter.

Place the chicken in a cast-iron casserole and pour the sauce over the top.

Fry the vegetables in a pan and add them to the chicken. Simmer for another two minutes and then serve the chicken from this casserole.

Fried potatoes can also be added to the casserole if you like.

Note:
- *Ask your butcher to cut the chicken 'for sauté'. That means that the backbone is removed first and then the chicken is cut into eight pieces: the butcher will remove the legs and cut them in half. After that he will cut the breast down the middle along the breast bone and then cut these pieces in two again.*
- *Make the brown chicken fond from the bones and neck of the poulet de Bresse.*
- *Buy preserved lemon or make it yourself by cutting the lemons into quarters, but leaving one end attached, and then marinating them for two to three weeks in a jar with 500 grams of sea salt, 100 grams of sugar and some water.*

CLASSIC DISHES

FILLET OF POULET DE BRESSE, ASPARAGUS, PEAS AND CHANTERELLE MUSHROOMS

INGREDIENTS

- 6 white asparagus ·
- 240 g (peeled weight) freshly shelled peas ·
- 4 *poulet de Bresse* fillets ·
- fat for frying ·
- salt and pepper to taste ·
- 8 butterhead lettuce leaves ·
- 2.5 ml flour ·
- pinch of icing sugar ·
- 12 fresh cocktail onions ·
- a few knobs of cold butter ·
- 120 g chanterelle mushrooms, wiped ·

Note:
Ask your butcher for a few chicken bones.

METHOD

Make a brown fond with the chicken bones.

Peel the asparagus and cut them diagonally into six pieces. Fry until crisp.

Blanch the peas.

Season the chicken fillets with salt and pepper. Fry them until crisp, starting with the skin side down. Finish them off in the oven at 200 °C for five to six minutes.

Prepare the peas the French way: braise the cocktail onions in butter then add the blanched peas and the lettuce leaves cut into long thin strips. Braise then sprinkle on 2.5 ml of flour and a pinch of icing sugar. Moisten with a little chicken fond and braise.

Add the asparagus.

Remove the chicken from the oven and deglaze the pan with the chicken fond. Boil down and enrich the sauce with a few knobs of butter.

Fry the chanterelle mushrooms.

Arrange the peas and the fried chanterelle mushrooms on the plate. Place the chicken next to them. Pour the sauce beside the chicken.

Preserved or fried potatoes go perfectly with this dish.

CLASSIC DISHES

CREAMY CHICKEN SOUP AND LOBSTER BISQUE

You will need 1 litre of soup for four people.

INGREDIENTS

- 600 g lobster
- 3 litre of court-bouillon
- 5 Tbsp. olive oil
- 800 ml strong chicken stock
- 1 clove of garlic
- 1 stick of celery, chopped
- 3 carrots, chopped
- thyme
- bay leaf
- 1/2 tsp. of flour
- 2 Tbsp. tomato purée
- a dash of cognac
- 50 ml white wine
- 300 ml fish fumet

- 3 onions, roughly chopped
- 3 leeks, white part only, in julienne
- 1 potato, roughly chopped

- 2 Tbsp. cream
- 4 shiitake mushrooms
- 100 g minced chicken
- a few sprigs of chervil

METHOD

Blanch the lobster in a court-bouillon. Remove the tail and the claws from the lobster and boil them for another four minutes. Chop the head in pieces and sauté in olive oil. Add the garlic, chopped carrots, celery, thyme and bay leaf and braise them for a moment. Sprinkle with half a tablespoon of flour; add two tablespoons of tomato purée and deglaze with a dash of cognac and the white wine. Cover with half of the fish fumet and half of the chicken fond. Leave to simmer gently for 20 minutes, then sieve the soup. Squeeze the liquid through well to give the soup as much flavour as possible.

Make chicken soup with the onions, the white part of the leeks, potato and the chicken stock. Blend the soup.

Combine the two soups (equal quantities of each). Add a little cream.

Dice the shiitake finely, sauté them and add them to the minced chicken. Make little meatballs of the mixture and blanch them.

Serve the soup in large, deep bowls. Arrange the lobster escallops and the meatballs in the bowl. Garnish with some sprigs of chervil.

CLASSIC DISHES

POZHARSKY MADE WITH POULET DE BRESSE, BRAISED CHICORY AND POMMES ANNA

INGREDIENTS

- 4 breast fillets from *poulet de Bresse*
- 10 g bone marrow/100 g chicken (net weight)
- 7 g white bread/100 g chicken (net weight)
- 100 ml cream
- 1 piece of fresh ginger
- salt, pepper and nutmeg to taste
- a pinch of sugar
- 1 kg Charlotte potatoes
- 100 g clarified butter
- 6 chicory stalks (not too big)

METHOD

Remove the skin from the chicken and cut off the wings. Wipe the wing bones clean and use the rest for the sauce.

Finely dice the white chicken, the bone marrow and the bread. Soak the bread in cream for a moment. Grate some ginger and mix with the chicken and bone marrow. Make four chicken cutlets from this forcemeat and coat with the breadcrumbs.

In the meantime, make the *pommes Anna*. Grease a cake tin with butter. Season with salt, pepper and a little nutmeg.

Peel the potatoes and slice them thinly into 2-millimetre slices using a mandolin. Dip the slices in the clarified butter and place them in the tin in the shape of a flower. Season each layer and repeat five times. Lay a butter paper over the top layer and place a weight on top so that the potatoes can bake under pressure for 20 minutes in the oven at 180 °C. Let the cake cool before removing the tin. You can heat the potato cake up again at a moment's notice.

Cut the chicory stalks down the middle and brown the cut side in a pan with some butter, salt, pepper, nutmeg and a pinch of sugar. Leave to caramelise, then turn them over and cook in a little water.

Fry the chicken cutlets in clarified butter for three minutes on each side. Stick the clean bones back in to make it look more like a cutlet.

Arrange the *pommes Anna,* the chicory and the chicken on plates.

Serve with brown chicken gravy.

CLASSIC DISHES

SALAD WITH BLOND CHICKEN LIVERS, COATED WITH SIROP DE LIÈGE AND GREEN BEANS

INGREDIENTS

For the pickle
- 237 g water
- 118 g rice vinegar
- 75 g sugar
- 12 g salt

- 320 g blond chicken livers from a *poulet de Bresse*
- 160 g green beans
- 160 g butter beans
- 1 large potato
- 1 Granny Smith
- 1 red onion
- 4 slices of dried bacon *(pancetta)*
- red radish or Japanese parsley *(optional)*
- Sirop de Liège to taste

*Note:
blond (fatty) chicken livers
are tastier than goose liver.*

METHOD

Preparation

First make the pickle. Boil the water, rice vinegar, sugar and salt together and then leave to cool. Cut the red onion into segments and pickle them.

Remove the gall and any membrane from the blond chicken livers.

Boil the two types of beans separately and then plunge them into ice water.

Peel the potato and cut in 1-cm dice. Cook them until just tender.

Cut the apple in the same way.

Dry the bacon on greaseproof paper.

Method

Split the beans and season with oil, vinegar, salt and pepper. Arrange them on a plate and place a few segments of pickled red onion on top.

Fry the potatoes quickly in butter. Arrange them on the plate with the cubes of apple.

Fry the chicken livers quickly in a pan; caramelise with the *sirop de Liège*. Arrange them on the plate.

Garnish with the dried bacon and the red radish or Japanese parsley.

Sans cravate, a restaurant where no ties are allowed.

→ Henk Van Oudenhove of restaurant Sans Cravate in Bruges.

Galantine, a classic French dish from Poland

There are times when you come across a stuffed chicken or rabbit in the better traditional delicatessens in French towns and villages and stare in amazement at the way it has been so skilfully deboned and then reformed into its more or less original form. This irresistible delicacy is called *galantine* and is a classic dish with Polish roots.

Galantine is indeed a Polish dish made from a completely deboned chicken or other animal, stuffed with a mixture of meat from both the animal in question and other animals. The forcemeat is shaped to resemble the animal and then poached or fried. This elegant piece of work is culminated by having aspic poured over it and being decorated with flowers, for example, or a hunting scene. It is a sophisticated dish that requires a huge amount of skill and time. The major difference between it and pâté is that galantine cannot be spread. It should not be confused with *galauntine* or *galantyne*. You frequently come across these terms in mediaeval cookery books but they mostly refer to sauces based on galangal root, breadcrumbs and cinnamon. These sauces used to be eaten with eel, goose and game.

Henk Van Oudenhove

Which chef in Belgium is crazy enough or passionate enough to make this very labour-intensive dish? There aren't many, but there is one 'last of the Mohicans' in Bruges. Presiding over a restaurant where you are not allowed to wear a tie, Sans Cravate, is the ever genial Henk Van Oudenhove.

Henk is a chef who is creating a distinct profile for himself while still keeping both feet on the ground. The skills in his kitchen go deep, sometimes flirting with contemporary fashion, sometimes with traditional methods. I have a sneaking suspicion that he feels most at home in the classic register, but that's only a hunch. He resolutely chooses the less obvious methods of preparation and cooking techniques. One example is his universally praised *galantine de volaille de Bresse*, an ode to Escoffier, and he is a magician with the spit. He is a seriously underrated chef who deserves more attention than he gets.

CLASSIC DISHES

POULET DE BRESSE 'EN GALANTINE'

INGREDIENTS

- 1 *poulet de Bresse*, 2 kg
- salt and pepper to taste
- 6 sheets of gelatine

For the forcemeat
- 150 g lean chicken, membrane and tendons removed
- 100 g lean pork, membrane and tendons removed
- 150 g pork fat *(preferably from the throat)*
- 1 chicken liver
- 1 slice of white bread, soaked in cream and milk
- 1 Tbsp. pistachios, roughly chopped
- 3 slices of smoked ham

For the stock
- 3 litres stock
- 39 g salt
- aromatics

For the chaud-froid
- 1.3 litres cream *(40% fat)*
- 30 g gelatine
- 20 g cornflour
- 50 ml dry white wine

To finish
- 2 onions
- 1 stick of celery
- 2 carrots
- 1 leek
- 2 cloves
- 2 bay leaves
- 2 hard-boiled eggs

Equipment
- thermometer
- trussing needle and string
- tea towel

METHOD

Debone the chicken very carefully, starting along the backbone, but leave the liver.

It is extremely important that you don't cut into the skin. (Otherwise it will tear when cooking and you will lose the smooth outer surface.)

Remove the inner carcass from the chicken but leave the chicken thigh bones in. (They will act as the backbone during poaching.)

Season with salt and pepper and then chill.

Farce

We season the meat with a mixture of herbs and spices (which you are best to mix yourself; you can then use the mixture for other dishes). I allow 16 grams per kilogram of forcemeat. Remember that it already contains salt.

Grind the fat only once and chill immediately.

Grind the lean chicken, pork and liver twice then chill.

Grind the soaked bread with the meat.

Place a bowl over some ice and carefully mix the ground fat into the ground meat three times.

Finish off with the chopped pistachios and chopped ham.

Taste to check the seasoning.

Stuff the chicken with the forcemeat trying to use the same quantity as the carcass you have removed and reform it into the same shape.

Close up the chicken again carefully and truss it securely from the bottom end to the neck with the needle and thread.

(continued on p. 164)

(continued from p. 162)

Be careful not to truss the chicken too tightly, but it is important that it is secure.

Tie up the chicken once more, forming it into the desired shape. Truss it in the same way you would if you were going to fry it.

Wrap the chicken carefully in a tea towel. (This is a crucial point: the way you secure the chicken in the tea towel will determine the way it comes out afterwards.)

In the meantime, put 3 litres of water, 39 grams of salt and the aromatics on to boil. Simmer for 10 minutes.

Carefully lower the wrapped chicken into the water and poach for two hours at 80 °C. Check the temperature of the water regularly with a thermometer.

Let the chicken cool in the pan overnight. Place a heavy weight on top to keep it under water, if necessary.

The next day

Carefully remove the chicken in the tea towel from the stock then remove the tea towel. Reserve the stock.

Rinse the chicken quickly under hot water and then pat dry with kitchen paper.

The hot water will help to rinse the fat off the chicken. Do this thoroughly, because the white chaud-froid won't stick if there is any fat remaining. Pat dry and place on a rack in a cool place.

Chaud-froid

Sieve the remaining stock and reduce two litres of it down to one litre.

In a separate pan, reduce the cream by half.

Combine the two liquids together after passing them through a fine sieve. Boil for a moment then dissolve the cornflour in white wine and add to the stock and cream. Bring back to the boil for a moment. Sieve and add the soaked gelatine.

Place a bowl containing 80% of the chaud-froid sauce over ice and turn it gently using a spatula to help it to cool (don't beat it at all – you don't want any air bubbles).

Keep the other 20% lukewarm to add to the rest of the sauce if it cools too much.

As soon as the chaud-froid on ice is the right temperature to stick, spread it generously over the chicken until it covers it completely. Chill.

Clarify the remaining chicken stock as if for consommé. Add 6 sheets of gelatine for each litre. Allow to set and then cut it into cubes to garnish the plate.

Decorate the chicken any way you like with cooked carrot, egg, leek and chives. Gently brush the consommé over the decorations (this prevents them from discolouring and drying out and makes them nice and shiny).

Add a seasonal salad garnish. The filling can also change with the seasons. (Fresh truffles or nuts in the forcemeat in the winter are always a success.)

Henk resolutely chooses the less obvious methods of preparation and cooking techniques. One example is his universally praised *galantine de volaille de Bresse*, an ode to Escoffier.

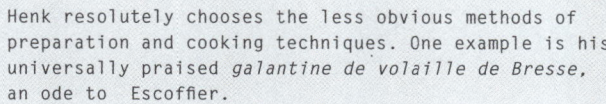

CLASSIC DISHES

CLASSIC DISHES

166

Steven Naessens
of restaurant Arbois.

Du vin d'Arbois, de plus on en boit, de plus on va droit

I can assure you that that is not true. Arbois has been a frequent culinary and vinous destination of mine for a long time. And I've been a regular patron of the restaurant Jean-Paul Jeunet for over 30 years. Jeunet is a respected and admired gastronomic family in Arbois and has been enormously significant for the cultural heritage of this region. I've actually been eating the same thing there for 30 years and I'm not planning on changing that now. I began to be treated like one of the family and they had a surprise for me in store in 2005. A shy man was summoned from the kitchen and introduced as *le Belge*.

Top of the pecking order

Steven Naessens comes from Bruges and spent two years working in the kitchen run by the absolute super star, Peter Goossens. That was until he swapped Kruishoutem in Belgium for Arbois in France in 2005 and began working for another legend. He soon rose to become sous chef and his wife became a pastry chef. From 2011 on it became clear that Jeunet was considering retiring. Steven sensed his opportunity and in due course took over the restaurant until Jeunet finally left the business in 2015.

Subtle changes are taking place which reveal Steven's powerful personality as both a chef and a businessman. One of the biggest crowd-pullers is a monumental dish that should feature on everyone's bucket list: *poulet au vin jaune et morilles*. It is a dish that sweeps you along into a vortex of tastes and emotions, before gently setting you down again. There are so many of those dishes that you can't get enough of; dishes that have the same effect as an inspiring artwork. As I say, I must have eaten this dish dozens of times and I eagerly look forward to it every time just as much as the last. It is some kind of addiction. Steven inherited this dish of course, but here too he has introduced subtle changes that add enormously to it and reveal his top-class abilities.

Steven is the only truly Belgian chef to have attained two Michelin stars on French soil, but apart from that, he is a chef who should be treasured, and visited again very soon.

Poulet de Bresse with vin jaune and morels

CLASSIC DISHES

POULET DE BRESSE WITH VIN JAUNE AND MORELS

INGREDIENTS

For the sauce poularde
- 2 poulardekarkassen ·
- 2 poularde carcasses ·
- 400 ml chicken stock ·
- 400 ml thick cream ·
- 300 ml Vin Jaune or Savagnin ·
- 800 g butter ·
- salt and pepper to taste ·

For the chicken thighs and stuffing
- 10 chicken thighs ·
- 100 g white meat, cut into 2-cm dice ·
- 25 g egg white ·
- 1 g pepper ·
- 3.5 g salt ·
- 500 ml cream ·
- 25 g morels, fried in nut oil + a few extra for the garnish ·

For the breasts and stuffing
- 10 chicken breasts ·
- 25 g blond livers, diced ·
- 1 Tbsp. nut oil or clarified butter ·
- 2 g garlic, finely chopped ·
- 10 g shallots, finely chopped ·
- 20 g chives, finely chopped ·
- 10 g of fresh pistachios ·
- 1 g curry powder ·

For the garnish
- 2 sticks of white celery in julienne 8 x 1.5 cm ·
- 100 ml olive oil ·
- 1 stick of celery ·
- 1 bunch of tarragon ·

METHOD

Sauce poularde

Put the *poularde* carcasses into a pan with the chicken stock and bring to the boil. Simmer on a low heat for eight hours, sieve and chill in the fridge. Remove the layer of fat and boil down until you are left with 200 ml.

Add the 400 ml of thick cream and 100ml of *Vin Jaune* or Savagnin.

Reduce until you are left with 300 ml; add 800 grams of good butter cut into cubes to thicken it, mix and add a few spoonfuls of *Vin Jaune*. Season to taste with salt and pepper.

Morels

Soak the morels for 48 hours in plenty of water. Drain and reduce the soaking liquid until there is just enough to heat up the morels in later on.

Chicken thighs and stuffing

Make sure that all these ingredients are well chilled.

Beat the white meat with the egg white and add the salt. Gradually add the cream and mix well. Add the morels and beat for at least 10 seconds.

Insert 20 grams of this mixture into the thigh as stuffing.

Breasts and stuffing

Sweat the blond livers in the nut oil for a few minutes. Remove from the heat.

Do the same with the garlic and the shallot; add the pistachios and set aside.

Add the chives and the curry powder and beat until smooth.

Fill the breasts with the mixture.

Garnish

Brown the white celery in olive oil; moisten with half a litre of chicken stock and cook on a low heat for an hour.

Use a mandolin to cut a few very thin slices from the celery. Blanch them in water for one minute. Brush them with oil, place them between two sheets of kitchen paper and dry them in the oven set to 70 °C for three hours.

Cook the rest of the celery in a litre of chicken stock for an hour; beat until you have a smooth puree.

To finish

Fry the chicken breasts and the chicken thighs in chicken fat; slice them and arrange on one side of a place. Lay some warmed morels on top.

Arrange the celery structures on the other side of the plate; garnish with some olive oil and tarragon leaves.

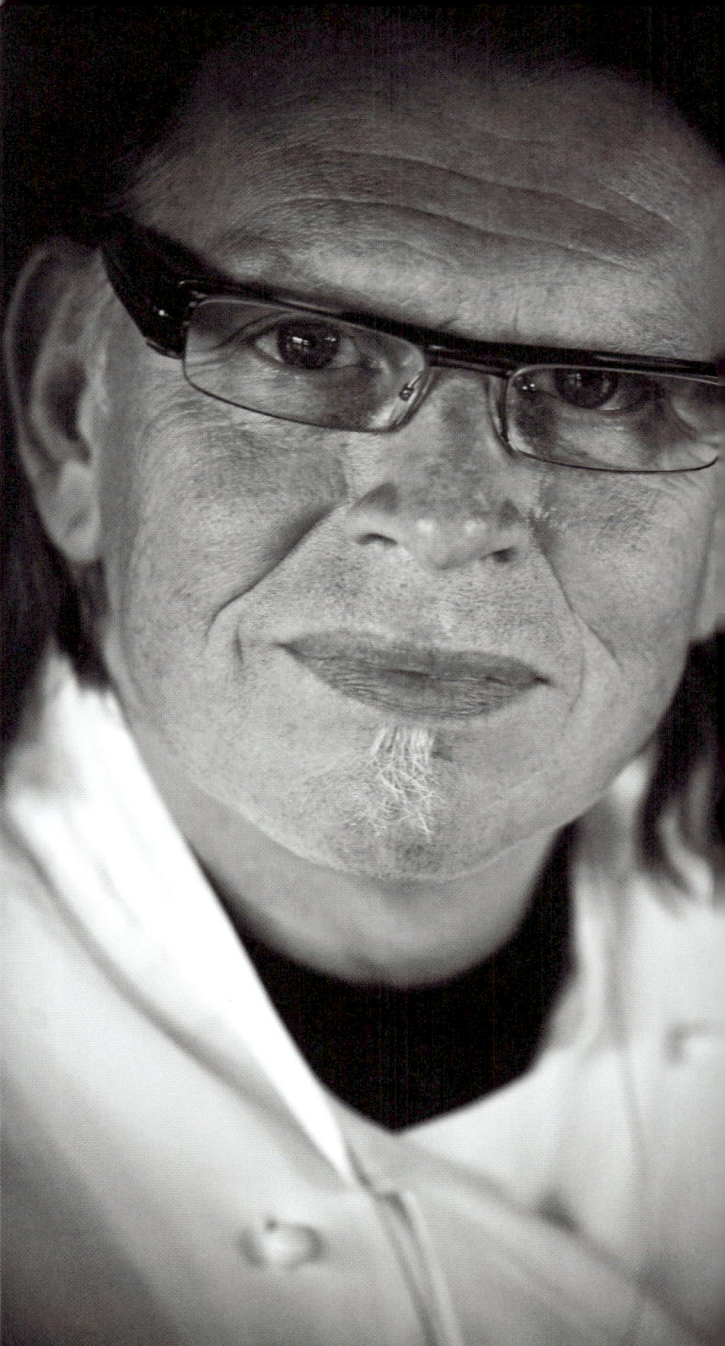

→ Just walking in to 't Fornuis is always a special experience, a time to rub your hands in delight at what is about to happen.

→ Johan Segers enjoys continuing the tradition in 't Fornuis.

A treasure trove in a national treasure

One of the most uncompromising chefs, and by extension, most uncompromising restaurants, in Belgium is Johan Segers and his restaurant 't Fornuis. Just walking in is always a special experience, a time to rub your hands in delight at what is about to happen. A restaurant of such high quality is of course the result of teamwork. And here is no exception. I have two reasons for visiting restaurants: sometimes I just feel like eating a vol-au-vent and so I go to X, and sometimes I feel like enjoying a particular style of cooking and then it doesn't really matter what the chef in questions prepares for me. And the latter is what takes me to 't Fornuis. Although they can make virtually anything, my favourite meal is chicken in any of its facets.

Chicken in a pig's bladder

An unusual technique is the *poularde en vessie*, or chicken cooked entirely in a sealed pig's bladder. This recipe was devised at the end of the 19th century by Françoise Fayolle (1865-1925), better known as la Mère Fillioux. She was undoubtedly the most important French chef of her generation and a fountain of inspiration for many who followed. She began her cookery career in the wine bar owned by her husband, Louis Fillioux, at 73, rue Duquesne in Lyon. Her talents turned this bistro into a place of pilgrimage for culinary connoisseurs. Later on, she became chef to Eugénie Brazier, better known as la Mère Brazier. Apart from being famous for her *poularde en vessie*, she is also considered to be the mother of the *poularde en demi deuil*, in which slices of truffles are inserted under the skin of a chicken; it is still served this way in the restaurant La Mère Brazier. Eugénie Brazier was incidentally the first female chef to ever receive three Michelin stars, which she did in 1933.

This recipe guarantees that the chicken is ultra-succulent and moist and it is simply unique.

Johan Segers

Johan Segers, Michelin-starred chef, businessman, ideal son-in-law, Harley rider, TV chef, author, philosopher… enjoys continuing the tradition in 't Fornuis Johan was the first devotee of the nouvelle cuisine movement. His kitchen is absolutely magnificent and averse to all trends. When I was a little boy playing football in the streets with my friends, his lovely wide front door often served as our goal. If we scored too often, his imposing, long-haired personage would appear and chase us away. We were a bit scared of this mild giant, because he is a giant, in all respects. We've made up since. Nowadays, the godfather of Belgian gastronomy seems to be even more dynamic than ever and preaches about the excellent cuisines of the past like a relentless missionary.

You develop your own vision and style at a young age, and talking to Johan is like looking at a major work of art. There is a deeper meaning, a longing to seek out the essence of every sentence he utters, of every brushstroke. Ballast overboard, masks off; purity and daring. His greatest secret is perhaps that there is no secret. Everything is inspiration. His philosophy is that you mustn't go to a place where everyone is trying to look for inspiration; take your inspiration from everyday things like a colourful, sweet-smelling market, a walk, a work of art, a book, a rock concert, an opera. Differences and contrasts enrich your life and therefore also your mentality and your fall-back base. You are your own source of inspiration. If you do nothing but cook, your life is empty, even if you treat an empty plate as your canvas. He is a true gentleman and a very special friend.

CLASSIC DISHES

CHICKEN IN PIG'S BLADDER

INGREDIENTS

1 pig's bladder ·
1 chicken, approx. 1.5 kg ·
50 ml port ·
50 ml cognac ·

For the cream sauce

20 ml port ·
20 ml cognac ·
100 ml chicken stock ·
1 Tbsp. glace de viande ·
0.5 litre cream ·
salt and pepper to taste ·

METHOD

Soak the bladder in cold water. Turn it inside out and rinse well.

Prepare the chicken for the pan. Season it with salt and pepper.

Make an incision in the bladder opening and insert the chicken. Add the port and the cognac. Fasten up the bladder with kitchen string, tying it round twice to make sure it is sealed.

Poach the chicken in the bladder in water for 1.5 hours, dousing it regularly so that the bladder does not dry out.

Sauce
Reduce the port and the cognac a little in a pan. Add the chicken stock and boil down until it has reduced by a third. Add the glace de viande and boil down until it has reduced by a third.

Add the cream and reduce to the thickness of a sauce. Season to taste.

Remove the chicken from the bladder, retaining the liquid, and cut the chicken in pieces.

Arrange on a plate and pour the sauce over.

The liquid from the bladder can be served separately in a small coffee cup.

Serve with morels, ceps or truffles if you like.

CLASSIC DISHES

FRESH PASTA WITH COCKSCOMBS, CHICKEN LIVER, STOMACH, HEART AND FRESH MORELS

INGREDIENTS

4 cockscombs ·
4 preserved chicken stomachs ·
12 preserved chicken hearts ·
coarse sea salt ·
3 sprigs of thyme ·
3 bay leaves ·
1 litre goose fat ·
salt ·
1 bouquet garni ·
200 g fresh pasta ·
breadcrumbs ·
oil for deep-frying ·
8 Tbsp. chicken stock ·
1 knob of butter ·
pepper ·
120 g fresh morels ·
4 chicken livers ·

METHOD

Rinse the cockscombs, chicken stomachs and hearts in cold water to remove all impurities, such as blood.

Dry the hearts and stomachs and mix them with a handful of coarse sea salt, thyme and bay leaves; mix well and put in the fridge to rest for 12 hours. After that, rinse them again thoroughly under running water to remove all the salt.

Cook the stomachs and hearts in melted goose fat with a dash of water over a gentle heat for four hours.

Bring the cockscombs to the boil in salted water.

Skim off the scum from the water and add the bouquet garni. Cook gently for two hours on a low heat. After that, remove the membrane from the combs by rubbing them.

Cook the pasta al dente in salted water.

Dip the cockscombs in breadcrumbs and deep-fry them in hot oil.

Chop the preserved stomachs and hearts; put them in a pan with some chicken stock, a knob of butter and some pepper. Add the washed and cleaned morels.

Bring to the boil for a moment, season to taste and mix them into the cooked pasta.

Fry the chicken livers at the last minute. Add them to the pasta with the fried cockscombs.

CLASSIC DISHES

FINANCIÈRE EN FEUILLETÉ AU BRUN

INGREDIENTS

1 chicken, approx. 1.5 kg ·
12 hard-boiled quails' eggs, halved ·
12 cockscombs ·
200 g minced meat ·
150 g veal sweetbreads ·
20 mushroom caps ·
knob of butter ·
1 large bouchée, puff pastry case ·

For the sauce
0.5 litre chicken stock ·
0.5 litre brown fond ·

METHOD

Brown the chicken in butter and cook in the oven at 175 °C for about 45 minutes.

Cook the cockscombs in the chicken stock for about an hour.

Dice the sweetbreads and poach them with the cockscombs.

Roll the minced meat into meatballs and poach them in salted water.

Braise the mushrooms in a knob of butter.

Sieve the stock containing the cockscombs and the sweetbreads, boil down with the brown fond until it resembles a sauce.

Chop the chicken and mix all the ingredients, season to taste and arrange in the bouchée.

CLASSIC DISHES

CHICKEN LIVER AND CRAYFISH FLAN

INGREDIENTS

For the flan
250 g chicken liver ·
1.5 egg white ·
25 ml cream ·
10 ml cognac ·
10 ml port ·
salt and pepper to taste ·

For the sauce
200 ml reduced bisque ·
100 ml cream ·
75 g cold butter ·

For the garnish
12 poached crayfish ·

METHOD

Flan

Blend all the ingredients in a blender until smooth then push through a sieve.

Butter 4 dariole moulds and fill them ¾ full.

Place them in a bain-marie in the oven at 175 °C for eight to nine minutes.

Rest for a moment then turn out.

Sauce

Bring the bisque to the boil.

Add the cream and simmer for a moment.

Whisk in the cold butter and season to taste.

Finish off with the peeled crayfish.

CLASSIC DISHES

CHICKEN SALAD WITH CEPS

INGREDIENTS

1 chicken, approx. 1.5 kg ·
12 quails' eggs ·
3 potatoes, sliced for frying ·
mixture of lettuce leaves ·
(butterhead lettuce, lamb's lettuce, rocket)
1 spring onion, finely chopped ·
1 Jonagold apple, julienned ·
6 walnuts, chipped ·
200 g fresh ceps, sliced ·

For the vinaigrette
50 ml olive oil ·
50 ml chardonnay vinegar ·
50 ml walnut oil ·
Salt and pepper ·

For the sauce
1 Tbsp. *glace de viande* ·
3 Tbsp. chicken stock ·

METHOD

Brown the chicken in butter and cook in the oven at 175 °C for about 45 minutes.

Fry the sliced potatoes in oil until golden.

Fry the ceps and season with salt and pepper.

Fry the quails' eggs in a moulded pan.

Mix the lettuce with the spring onion, apple and the chopped nuts and dress with the vinaigrette.

Slice the chicken thinly.

Remove the skin and bake it in the oven until crisp.

Deglaze the pan with the chicken stock and the glace de viande.

Sieve.

Season to taste with salt and pepper.

Place a little chicken on the plate and then top it alternately with the other ingredients. Add a few spoonfuls of sauce. Finish off with the crisp skin.

Additional garnish: preserved chicken stomachs and hearts

Real cooking with real ingredients!

Tafeltje Rond, a traditional brasserie, is Filip's new home.

→ Filip Slangen, truly at home in the kitchen, has a wide-ranging repertoire of wonderful dishes, most of which have a traditional streak.

Filip Slangen

Filip worked as a magician's apprentice under the classic Belgian masters, Johan Segers and Wouter Keersmaeckers. The three of them attained a second Michelin star for 't Fornuis.

Filip was still only very young when he started working at this establishment and he became fascinated by Segers' methods, which were quite avant-garde at the time. Truly at home in the kitchen, Filip has a wide-ranging repertoire of wonderful dishes, most of which have what we would call a traditional streak. After leaving 't Fornuis, he went in search of success as a domestic caterer but the call of the wild in the form of serving customers was too strong and so he recently opened what he himself calls a classic brasserie.

Real cooking with real ingredients is his passion and is what drives him. Slangen is an underrated chef who likes to take you with him on his culinary adventure visiting meticulously finished, rich, classic dishes on the way.

Cooking with Babette

There are few films that can make your mouth water, but *Babette's Feast* is one. When I watch the scene where Babette makes the *caille en sarcophage* and unites the whole village, I salivate so much that I have to change my T-shirt.

The Café Anglais was a famous French restaurant at the corner of the Boulevard des Italiens and the Rue de Marivaux in Paris. It opened in 1802 and its name is a tribute to the Treaty of Amiens which brought peace between the British and the French in that same year. It was originally a working-class haunt but later, as more and more actors and opera singers began to frequent it, its fame grew. Paul Chevreuil revamped it in 1822, turning it into a glitzy hip restaurant serving mostly grilled and fried meat. With the arrival of the chef, Adolphe Dugléré, Café Anglais became a true gastronomic reference point, frequented by the aristocracy and beau monde of Paris. His creations included *pommes Anna* in honour of Anne Deslions, *soupe Germiny* and *caille en sarcophage*. The restaurant closed in 1913 but it left its mark in many ways... The main character in Babette's Feast had been a chef in Café Anglais before she fled to Denmark before the war.

If *caille en sarcophage* gives people so much pleasure, can't we increase that pleasure by making the bird bigger? Filip Slangen thought that must be possible and created *poussin en sarcophage*.

CLASSIC DISHES

COQ AU VIN

INGREDIENTS

- 1 good quality roasting chicken
- 300 ml red wine
- 1 large carrot
- 1 onion
- 1 clove of garlic
- 1 bay leaf
- a few sprigs of thyme
- 1 Tbsp. goose fat
- 200 g streaky bacon, in strips
- 0.5 kg mushrooms
- cocktail onions
- 100 ml demi-glace sauce
- roux
- salt and pepper to taste

METHOD

Debone the chicken and cut the breast and legs in two. Marinate them in a good red wine to which you have added the chopped carrot, the onion, the garlic, the bay leaf and the thyme.

Put in the fridge for 24 hours.

Remove the chicken from the marinade, drain it well and then dredge it with flour.

Fry the pieces of chicken in a tablespoonful of goose fat in a saucepan until they are nicely browned. Remove the well-browned pieces of chicken from the pan.

Put the strips of bacon, the mushroom caps, the cocktail onions and the vegetables from the marinade into the saucepan and braise them.

Return the chicken to the pan and moisten everything with the marinade.

Add the demi-glace sauce and cook for about 10 minutes without a lid.

If necessary, thicken the sauce with the roux. Season to taste with salt and pepper.

CLASSIC DISHES

ROAST CHICKEN WITH LEMON AND ROSEMARY

INGREDIENTS

- 1 chicken
- 1 clove of garlic
- fleur de sel
- rosemary
- 1 lemon
- piment d'Espelette

METHOD

Cut the chicken up according to the crapaudine (also known as spatchcock or butterfly) method: cut the chicken along the backbone and remove the carcass. Now turn the chicken over and flatten it so that the thighs lie next to the breast. Fasten it in place with 2 skewers.

Put a clove of garlic in a mortar with the fleur de sel, the piment d'Espelette, the rosemary and lemon rind. Crush everything until fine. Spread this mixture over the chicken and leave to marinate for a few hours.

Grill the chicken until cooked.

Serve with roast vegetables.

CLASSIC DISHES

POUSSIN EN SARCOPHAGE

INGREDIENTS

- 1 spring chicken
- 1 piece of goose liver weighing approx. 40 g
- a few strips of black truffle
- a sheet of puff pastry
- egg yolk to brush the pastry
- 1 shallot
- dash of cognac and port
- 4 large mushrooms
- 100 ml demi-glace sauce

METHOD

Debone the spring chicken and stuff it with a nice piece of goose liver and a slice of black truffle.

Form the sheet of pastry into an oval pastry case, brush with the egg yolk and bake as you would as you would when making a vol-au-vent.

Fry the spring chicken in butter and then cook it in the oven for about 15 minutes, depending on its weight.

Remove the chicken from the casserole, place it in the puff pastry case and keep it warm in the oven.

Fry the large mushroom caps in the same pan. Remove them from the pan and keep them warm.

Braise the chopped shallot in the same pan and moisten with the cognac, port and demi-glace sauce. Season to taste with salt and pepper, sieve and add the strips of black truffle. Stir in a knob of butter at the last minute.

Place the filled pastry case on a plate, pour the sauce over and finish off with the mushrooms.

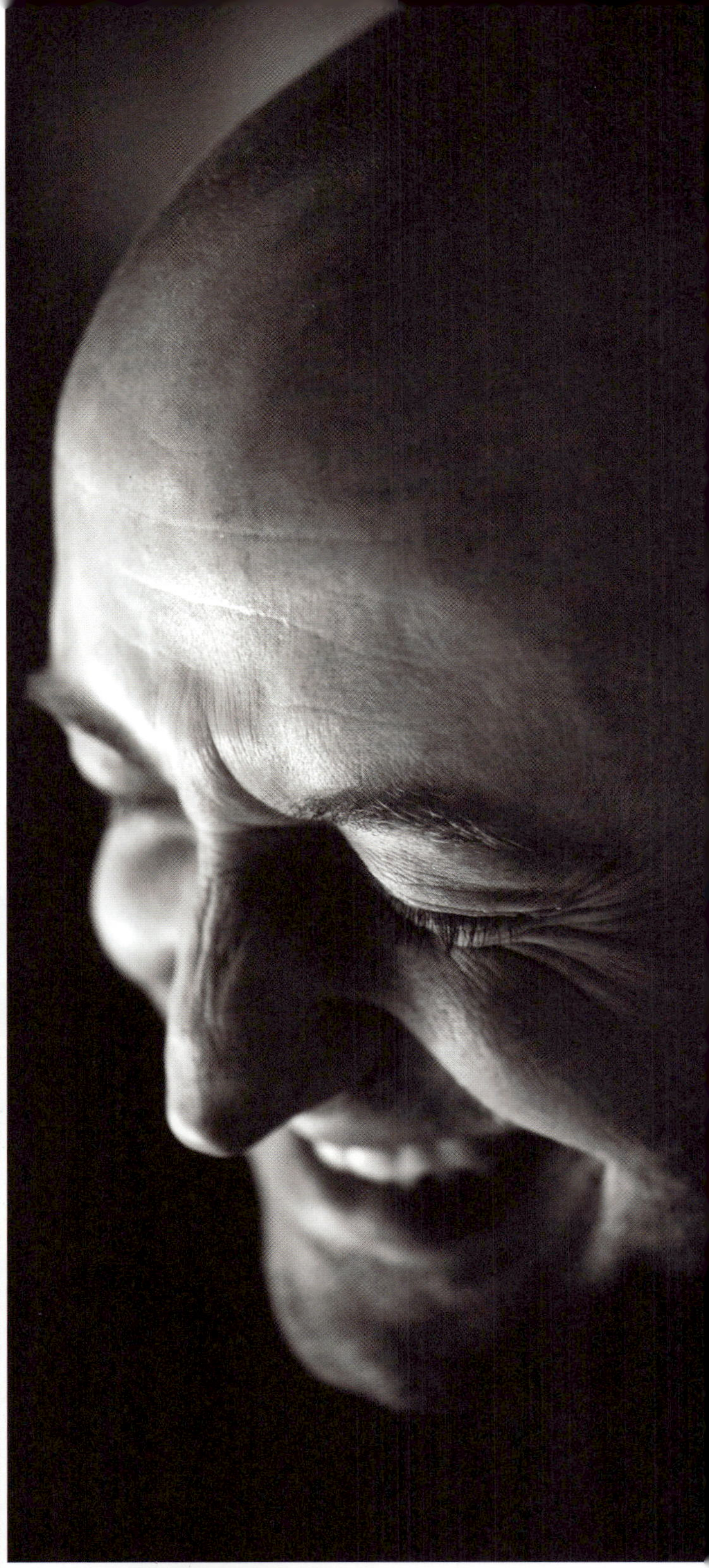

LA PAIX
BRUXELLES BRUSSEL

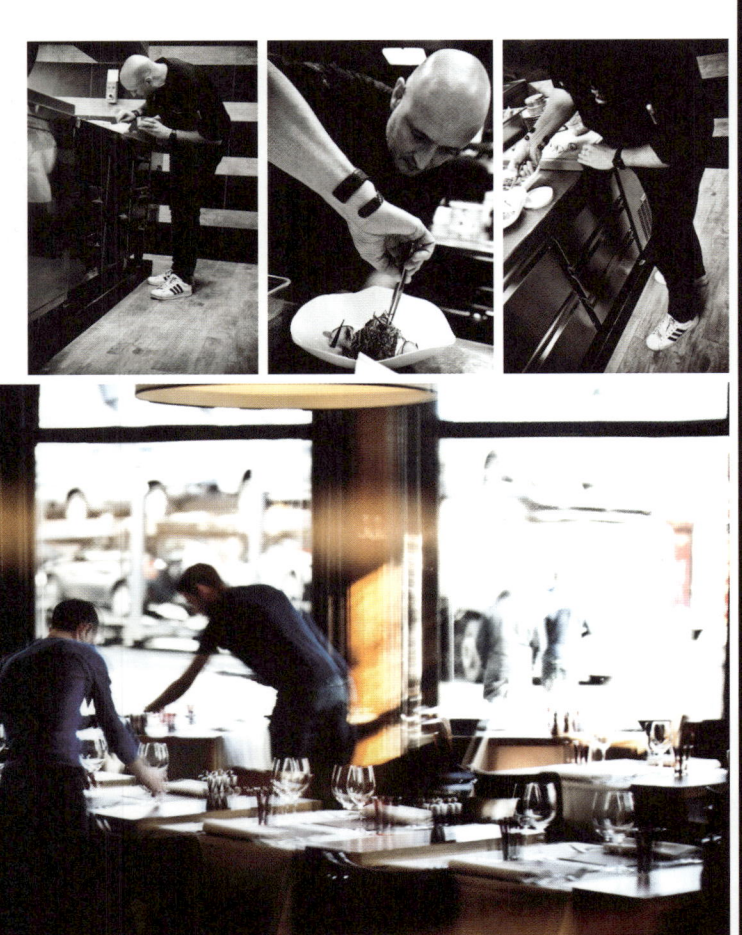

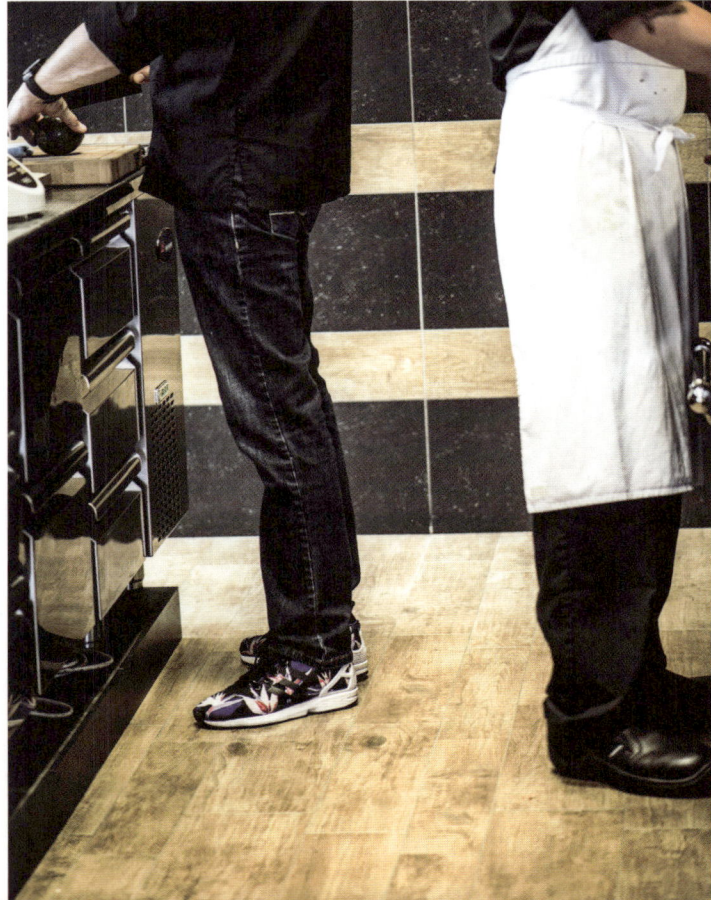

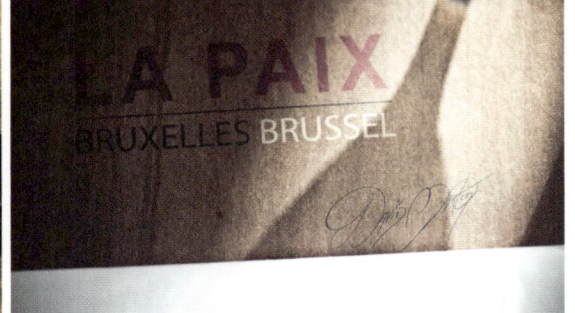

→ David Martin's flexibility and knowledge as a chef and as a businessman are exemplary.

David Martin

A chef like David Martin is exceptional. He has the flexibility I have seldom seen in a chef and that is an exceptional quality. At the age of 35, he decided he had seen enough at Bruneau and took over the kitchen in the restaurant owned by his parents-in-law, La Paix in Brussels. Not entirely unexpectedly, he put all his experience from the Michelin-starred restaurant at the complete disposal of the elegant, simpler brasserie kitchen and surprised friends and foes with his vision of brasserie classics. Many chefs think of themselves as revolutionary – goodness knows why. Here, the keyword is not revolution, but evolution. Refinement and a focus on flavour is what counts. To an outsider, it might sometimes seem that David is going in all sorts of different directions, but when all the pieces of the puzzle come together, it turns out that everything fits together nicely to form the bigger picture. *I love it when a plan comes together…*

When I was able to send David on a mission to Japan for the first time, something unexpected happened. After a breath-taking week he returned to his kitchen and began questioning everything. Japan had made a huge impression on him: his trip had been a true life-changing experience.

David began to immerse himself in Japanese cuisine like someone possessed: not just the technical aspects of food preparation but also the whole culture that surrounds it. He had quickly come to realise that it isn't the ingredients that determine the quality, but the philosophy of the chef. And so it wasn't only his vision of food that underwent 'Japanification', but the whole caboodle. He got rid of almost half of the available seating. Fewer guests so that he could look after people properly down to the last detail and could almost personalise their plates, as in the great *kaiseki* temples in the land of the rising sun. A second visit to Japan confirmed his feelings completely. David is a chef who is brave enough to break completely with a comfortable situation (a restaurant filled to capacity every day) and place himself in a vulnerable position once more. No one had expected this transformation. David's flexibility and knowledge as a chef and as a businessman are exemplary. He is a phenomenal talent who quietly pursues the strategy he has chosen, averse to trends and fashion fads; someone who has discovered his own style and determinedly embraces it. At a time when copying each other's discoveries seems to receive the most attention, David is refreshingly different. A type of chef threatened with extinction.

CLASSIC DISHES

FUCK YOU CHICKEN
AKA POULET DE BRESSE WITH GRILLED AUBERGINE AND ROAST CAULIFLOWER

INGREDIENTS

- 1 *poulet de Bresse*
- 1 organic lemon, cut into large pieces
- 1 handful of sage
- 50 g Picholine olives
- salted butter to taste

- a few vine leaves
- 2 aubergines, preferably from Sicily
- salt and pepper to taste
- 1 baby cauliflower (from Brittany)
- 20 fresh bay leaves
- 1 fresh bulb of garlic (from Gers)
- 1 chili pepper
- 200 g salted butter
- 1 tsp. dried chicken skin powder
- 0.5 litre concentrated chicken stock

METHOD

Remove the giblets from the chicken and stuff it with the lemon, sage, olives and the salted butter.

Tie the chicken up and braise it in a cast-iron casserole for 40 minutes with the lid on.

Take the lid off for the last five minutes and add the vine leaves to imbue the chicken with their scent. Leave the chicken to rest for 10 minutes.

Grill the aubergines on charcoal until the skin is dark brown; season them with salt and pepper and blend until creamy. Place the cauliflower in a casserole, stick the bay leaves into it and add the garlic and the chili pepper. Cover with the softened butter and the dried chicken skin powder. Roast the cauliflower for one hour at 200 °C.

Serve the chicken with the aubergine cream and the cooking gravy with pieces of lemon, the olives and the concentrated chicken. Serve the cauliflower separately, keeping it whole.

CLASSIC DISHES

SOT-L'Y-LAISSE (CHICKEN OYSTERS) WITH PRESERVED GARLIC

INGREDIENTS

300 g chicken oysters ·

For the sauce
10 cloves of garlic ·
200 ml sunflower oil ·
150 g dashi ·
2 tsp. dark soy sauce ·

METHOD

Marinate the garlic cloves in sunflower oil for an hour and a half until they are light brown in colour. Puree the garlic.

Pour a little garlic oil into a pan and add 50 g of the garlic puree; fry briskly for three minutes stirring continuously.

Deglaze with the dashi and the soy sauce and cook for five minutes more over a gentle heat. Pour in two soup spoonfuls of the remaining garlic oil and put the lid on.

To finish
Fry the chicken oysters for three to four minutes in a non-stick pan over a high heat, deglaze generously with the garlic sauce and leave for another five minutes.

Serve with some steamed rice and sprinkle with furikake.

CLASSIC DISHES

CHICKEN MARINATED IN SHIO KOJI AND GRILLED OVER CHARCOAL

INGREDIENTS

- 1 nice chicken ·
- salt to taste ·
- 200 g *shio koji* ·
- 1 pak choi ·
- 3 Tbsp. white soy sauce ·

For the dashi
- 100 g *kombu* leaf *rijiri* premium ·
- 350 g *katsuoboshi* ·
- 8 litres of water ·

METHOD

Dashi

Place the kombu in cold water and bring up to 80 °C; leave to infuse for 10 minutes. Add the katsuobushi and infuse for five minutes; increase the temperature to 85 °C and infuse for another five minutes before filtering.

Chicken

Debone the chicken by way of the backbone so that you retain everything in one piece. Season with salt and rub the skin side and the meat side with the shio koji.

Cover and leave for two days, in a vacuum bag if possible.

Remove the chicken from the bag. Leave the excess marinade on the chicken; it will caramelise and give the chicken the characteristic flavour this technique produces.

Grill the chicken on charcoal or, if that is not possible, in very little fat in a pan on a high heat.

To make the sauce, pour 200 ml of dashi into a pan, add the finely chopped pak choi and boil for five5 minutes.

Beat until very smooth, sieve and season with the white soy sauce.

Spoon some sauce onto a plate and arrange the cut chicken with the skin upwards.

CLASSIC DISHES

CHICKEN IN A COCOA AND COFFEE CRUST

INGREDIENTS

1 nice chicken

For the perfumed salt
2 tsp. dried rosemary ·
1 tsp. pimento de la vera (Spanish smoked paprika) ·
1 clove of garlic ·
1 tsp. of freshly ground coffee ·
100 g fine salt ·

For the crust
2 kg coarse grey sea salt ·
2 Tbsp. flour ·
4 Tbsp. cocoa ·
1 Tbsp. freshly ground coffee ·
5 egg whites ·

METHOD

Mix together all the ingredients for the perfumed salt.

Mix all the ingredients for the crust, starting with the dry ingredients and finishing with the egg whites.

Place a sheet of greaseproof paper on the baking tray and lay the crust mixture on it to a depth of two centimetres. Rub the perfumed salt into the chicken and place the chicken on the crust mixture.

Cover the chicken with the mixture, trying to keep it even. Place in a pre-heated oven (200 °C) and cook for an hour and 15 minutes. Remove from the oven and leave to rest for 15 minutes.

Break the crust when the chicken is on the table to release the aromas.

CLASSIC DISHES

WHOLE CHICKEN POACHED IN ARTISAN BUTTER

INGREDIENTS

1 good chicken of your choice ·
(poulet de Bresse, Maline chicken, guinea fowl)
3.5 kg artisan butter ·

Herbs for stuffing the chicken
1 clove of garlic ·
1 fresh chili pepper ·
2 sprigs of thyme ·
1 sprig of rosemary ·
1 pinch of nutmeg ·
1 small Cevenne onion ·
salt and pepper ·
100 ml thick raw cream ·
1 tsp. Vin Jaune ·

METHOD

The principle of cooking a chicken by total immersion is simple but requires certain accuracy.

Mix all the ingredients for seasoning the chicken and stuff the chicken with them. Tie up the chicken carefully so that the stuffing stays in while the chicken is cooking.

Choose a pan of the right size for the chicken so that you can measure out the right amount of butter.

Melt the butter to no more than 75 °C; do not exceed that temperature. Submerge the chicken in it for two hours, keeping the temperature at 75 °C. Calculate one hour's cooking time for each kilogram of chicken.

Remove the chicken and drain off the butter so that you can retain the chicken gravy and the whey at the bottom of the pan.

Pour that into a saucepan, mix with the thick cream and boil gently for five minutes; add a teaspoon of Vin Jaune if you like.

Slice the chicken and distribute over the plates, pour the creamy sauce over the top and serve with *aligot* if liked.

Chicken on a spit

Can there be anything more pleasing to a poultry lover than the smell of a high-quality roast chicken? I doubt it... It is always a delight and although roasting a chicken on a spit might seem easy, that is certainly not the case. There is no purer way of eating, or more delicious for that matter. The crisp skin followed by a mouthful of perfect chicken thigh is enough to smooth anyone's ruffled feathers. A spoonful of homemade tartar sauce finishes it off nicely.

I met Geert Vermeulen one rainy Wednesday in the market in Knokke. I couldn't believe my eyes or my ears. Geert is one of those people you can't be indifferent about; a man who lives for the market, who lives for his very distinctive poultry stall.

Most stalls stick to selling cut-price chickens that were cooked several hours ago and taste primarily of the cheapest chicken seasoning imaginable. Ghastly. But Het Gouden Haantje is different. Geert cooks *poulet de Bresse,* Malines, Muscovy ducks, *pigeon de Bresse,* spring chickens, French turkey thighs, organic chickens, guinea fowl and his phenomenal home-bred chickens, simply seasoned with a little salt and pepper and served as soon as they are perfectly cooked.

The passion and dedication of wonderful people like Geert are quite moving. He understands the trick of turning a simple ingredient into a work of art and, by choosing to sell his wares at the market, he is self-effacing too: no ego, no name on his white chef's design jacket. Respect!

I can stand hypnotised for hours watching the rotisserie steadily rotate as it gently turns various species of birds into golden delicacies. In the meantime, we have moved on to Antoine Westermann's simple 'bistrotisserie' in the heart of Paris. This pimped, simple rotisserie resembles a luxury chalet in St Anton, but the highest mountain near here is the butte of Montmartre.

Chicken is the order of the day here. Often the humblest dishes are the most difficult to reproduce while constantly maintaining the same high quality. Roast chicken with chips and salad is quite simply the touchstone here, the standard that should be filed away beside the platinum bar that serves as the benchmark for one metre at the International Bureau of Weights and Measures. This is a benchmark for chicken and chips with salad.

The various species of birds continue to troop past before my eyes as if on a revolving catwalk. For a moment I think about the other side of the street, where the legendary Moulin de la Galette is and where in days gone by Parisian beauties danced the cancan. *Pintade fermière d'Auvergne, poulet patte noire de Challans, poulet fermier du Maine, poulet de Bresse, pigeon du Poitou,* and so on. These are difficult times for people who like to taste and try things, because which honourable foodie wouldn't love to compare a *poulet de Bresse* with a *poulet de Challons*?

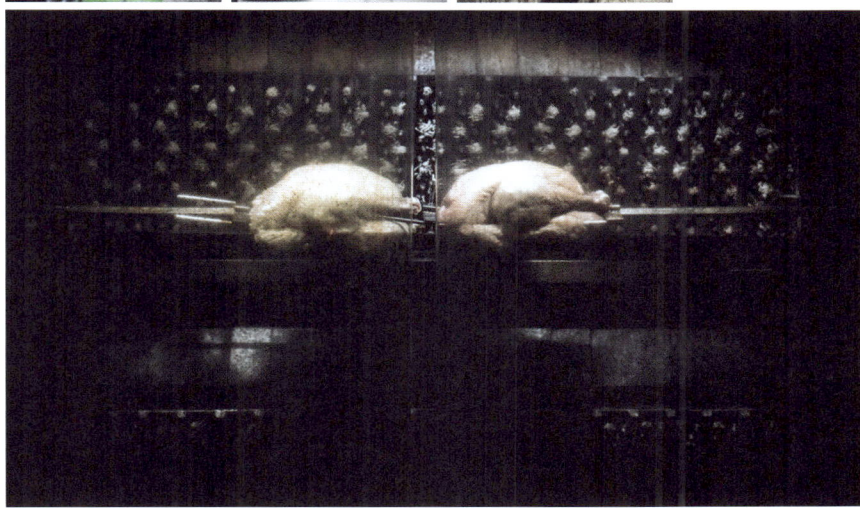

ADDRESSES

de Gulle Waard
Meester A.th. ten Houtenlaan 4
NL - 7102 EH Winterswijk
+31 543 513 133

Rossi
Standonckstraat 2
BE - 3000 Louvain

Osteria Francescana
Via Stella, 22
IT - 41121 Modena MO
+39 059 223912

Torigen
Shin-Yokohama prince Hall 2, 3F, 2-5-24
Shinyokohama
Kouhoku-ku
Yokohama-shi
JP - Kanagawa
+81 3 222-0033

Akira Yakitori
Marunouchi Brick Square
B1 2-6-1 Marunouchi
Chiyoda,
JP - Tokyo 100-6990,
+81 3-6269-9226

Dim Dining
Leeuwenstraat 1
BE - 2000 Antwerp
+32 3 226 26 70

Mmei - 5 flavors
Volkstraat 37
BE - 2000 Antwerp
+32 3 281 30 37

Jinjuu
Kingly Court, 15 Kingly St
GB - London W1B 5PS
+44 20 8181 8887

Shirkhan (Foodhalls)
Bellamyplein 51
NL - 1053 AT Amsterdam

Izakaya
Albert Cuypstraat 2-6
NL - 1072 CT Amsterdam
+31 020 305 3090

Dinner
Mandarin Oriental Hyde Park London
66 Knightsbridge
GB - London SW1X 7LA
+44 20 7201 3833

Sail&Anchor
Guldenvliesstraat 60
BE - 2600 Berchem
+32 3 430 40 04

Black Smoke
Mechelsesteenweg 291
BE- 2018 Antwerp

Caracas
Paardenmarkt 41
BE- 2000 Antwerp
+32 3 232 89 51

Brasserie Dock's
Jordaenskaai 7
BE - 2000 Antwerp
+32 3 226 63 30

Sans Cravate
Langestraat 159
BE - 8000 Bruges
+32 50 67 83 10

Jean-Paul Jeunet
9 Rue de l'Hôtel de ville
FR - 39600 Arbois
+33 3 84 66 05 67

't Fornuis
Reyndersstraat 24
BE - 2000 Antwerp
+32 3 233 62 70

Tafeltje Rond
Peperstraat 14
BE - 9120 Beveren
+32 468 30 13 10

La Paix
Rue Ropsy Chaudron 49
BE - 1070 Brussels
+32 2 523 09 58

`t Gouden Haantje
Wednesday and Saturday market
on Gemeenteplein, Knokke

Coq Rico
98 Rue Lepic
FR - 75018 Paris
+33 1 42 59 82 89

www.lannoo.com
Register on our website and we will send you regular newsletters containing information about new books and interesting, exclusive offers.

Publication details

Text: Luc Hoornaert

Photography: Kris Vlegels
(except for p. 8 and p. 146 top right and at the bottom of the page: Brasserie Dock's, p. 166: Restaurant Arbois and p. 167: Karmen Ayvazyan)

p 4: Mechelse Wyandotte – 20th Generation Cosmopolitan Chicken Project © Koen Vanmechelen

Design: Grietje Uytdenhouwen

Translation: Kay Dixon

If you have any comments or questions, please contact our editorial office: redactielifestyle@lannoo.com.

© Uitgeverij Lannoo nv, Tielt, Belgium - 2017
D/2017/45/94 – NUR 440-442
ISBN: 978-94-014-3771-4

All rights reserved. No part of this publication may be reproduced, stored in a retrieval system and/or published in any form or by any means, whether electronic, mechanical or otherwise without the prior permission in writing of the publisher.